LEARN SCIKIT-LEARN

Essential Machine Learning for Data Science

Diego Rodrigues

LEARN Scikit-Learn
Essential Machine Learning for Data Science

2025 Edition

Author: Diego Rodrigues

studiod21portoalegre@gmail.com

Published by StudioD21.

Important Note

The codes and scripts presented in this book have the main objective of illustrating, in a practical way, the concepts discussed throughout the chapters. They were developed to demonstrate teaching applications in controlled environments, and may therefore require adaptations to function correctly in different contexts. It is the reader's responsibility to validate the specific settings of their development environment before practical implementation.

More than providing ready-made solutions, this book seeks to encourage a solid understanding of the fundamentals covered, promoting critical thinking and technical autonomy. The examples presented should be seen as starting points for the reader to develop their own solutions, original and adapted to the real demands of their career or projects. True technical competence arises from the ability to internalize essential principles and apply them in a creative, strategic and transformative way.

We therefore encourage each reader to go beyond simply reproducing the examples, using this content as a basis to build codes and scripts with their own identity, capable of generating a significant impact on their professional career. This is the spirit of applied knowledge: learning deeply to innovate with purpose.

We thank you for your trust and wish you a productive and inspiring study journey.

CONTENTS

GREETINGS

It is with great enthusiasm that I welcome you to explore the powerful functionalities and advanced features of the Scikit-Learn library. Your decision to master Scikit-Learn clearly reflects a commitment to your professional growth and the pursuit of excellence in Data Science and Machine Learning, areas that are fundamental for driving intelligent, results-oriented solutions in today's world.

In this book, "LEARN Scikit-Learn – Essential Machine Learning for Data Science: From Fundamentals to Practical Applications," you will find a structured and comprehensive approach, designed to offer a solid learning experience that is fully applicable to the real-world challenges faced by data scientists and analysts today. Each chapter has been carefully built, starting from fundamental concepts to advanced practical examples, ensuring that you acquire not only the necessary theoretical knowledge but also the practical skill to implement real and highly efficient solutions using Scikit-Learn.

By dedicating yourself to this study, you prepare to face the challenges present in today's digital market, where mastering efficient Machine Learning techniques, rigorous model validation, optimized data management, and practical integration with other technologies are determining factors for the success of any technological project. Whether you are an experienced professional seeking to further enhance your skills or someone taking the first steps into the world of data science and machine learning, this book will provide a solid foundation and a broad view of the practical applications of this essential library.

Each chapter of this book has been meticulously crafted following the TECHWRITE 2.2 protocol, prioritizing absolute clarity, technical precision, and immediate applicability. You will learn from essential fundamentals, such as installation and configuration of the development environment with Python and Scikit-Learn, to more advanced techniques, including data preprocessing, feature engineering, regression and classification algorithms, ensemble methods, clustering techniques, dimensionality reduction, anomaly detection, automated pipelines, fine-tuning hyperparameters, and practical deployment of models into production.

At every stage of the proposed journey, you will find detailed explanations, carefully tested practical examples, as well as a section specifically dedicated to common errors, recommended solutions, essential best practices, and real-world applications, enabling a direct, fluid, and fully results-focused learning experience.

In today's highly competitive and data-driven context, mastering Scikit-Learn will provide you with a significant advantage, empowering you to build robust solutions capable of generating valuable insights, optimizing strategic decisions, and ensuring consistent performance in your Machine Learning applications.

Prepare for a deep, detailed, and, above all, practical journey. By the end of this book, you will be fully equipped to use Scikit-Learn in projects of any complexity, delivering effective results aligned with the best practices recognized worldwide.

Together, let's explore the essential and advanced functionalities of Scikit-Learn, clarify crucial concepts to master its tools, and transform your technical knowledge into real results. This is your moment to elevate your technical competence and ensure you stay ahead in a digital landscape that demands constant innovation and practical mastery of cutting-edge technologies.

Welcome, and enjoy your reading!

ABOUT THE AUTHOR

Diego Rodrigues
Technical Author and Independent Researcher
ORCID: https://orcid.org/0009-0006-2178-634X
StudioD21 Smart Tech Content & Intell Systems
E-mail: studiod21portoalegre@gmail.com
LinkedIn: www.linkedin.com/in/diegoxpertai

International technical author (tech writer) focused on structured production of applied knowledge. He is the founder of StudioD21 Smart Tech Content & Intell Systems, where he leads the creation of intelligent frameworks and the publication of technical books supported by artificial intelligence, such as the Kali Linux Extreme series, SMARTBOOKS D21, among others.

Holder of 42 international certifications issued by institutions such as IBM, Google, Microsoft, AWS, Cisco, META, Ec-Council, Palo Alto, and Boston University, he works in the fields of Artificial Intelligence, Machine Learning, Data Science, Big Data, Blockchain, Connectivity Technologies, Ethical Hacking, and Threat Intelligence.

Since 2003, he has developed more than 200 technical projects for brands in Brazil, the USA, and Mexico. In 2024, he established himself as one of the leading technical book authors of the new generation, with over 180 titles published in six languages. His work is based on his proprietary TECHWRITE 2.2 applied technical writing protocol, aimed at scalability, conceptual precision, and practical applicability in professional environments.

BOOK PRESENTATION

The current landscape of Data Science and Machine Learning has never been more dynamic and crucial to the success of organizations. With growing volumes of data and the urgent need for intelligent and automated solutions, mastering effective tools such as Scikit-Learn has become indispensable for professionals seeking excellence and consistent results. This book, "LEARN Scikit-Learn – Essential Machine Learning for Data Science: From Fundamentals to Practical Applications," was created to be your definitive guide, accompanying you from basic concepts to practical implementation in real-world scenarios.

Our journey begins in Chapter 1, with a comprehensive introduction to Scikit-Learn, presenting its history, evolution, and importance in data science, highlighting its modular architecture and how it differentiates itself from other Machine Learning libraries.

In Chapter 2, we set up the development environment, installing Python and Scikit-Learn, creating your first Machine Learning project, and running initial tests to ensure a fully functional environment.

We advance in Chapter 3 by exploring in detail the structure and fundamental concepts of the library, clarifying the importance of components, templates, metadata, and structural directives. Additionally, we discuss the role of Python within the Scikit-Learn context.

Chapter 4 dives deep into estimators, the essential components for building predictive models, introducing fundamental basic algorithms for practical understanding of Machine Learning.

Chapter 5 addresses essential data preprocessing techniques, such as scaling, normalization, and handling missing data, fundamental to ensuring the quality and effectiveness of the models created.

In Chapter 6, you will learn about Feature Engineering, including advanced techniques for feature creation, transformation, and selection, preparing robust data to boost your models' performance.

In Chapter 7, we present the regression models available in Scikit-Learn, detailing from linear regression to more advanced nonlinear techniques, essential for forecasting and quantitative data analysis.

Next, in Chapter 8, we cover the most important classification models, explaining and demonstrating essential algorithms for complex categorization problems, such as Logistic Regression, Decision Trees, and other fundamental methods.

In Chapter 9, you will learn about essential cross-validation techniques and detailed model evaluation, ensuring robustness and precision in the results obtained.

Chapter 10 deals with hyperparameter optimization, teaching how to effectively tune models to maximize their predictive performance.

In the subsequent chapters, we delve into advanced techniques essential for the complete Machine Learning professional: Chapter 11 explores ensemble methods, such as Random Forest and Gradient Boosting, which offer excellent accuracy and robustness; Chapter 12 presents a detailed introduction to Support Vector Machines (SVM), addressing their practical use and the contexts in which they best apply.

In Chapter 13, we work with simple neural networks through

Scikit-Learn's MLPClassifier, providing a solid foundation for basic and effective neural models.

Chapter 14 covers clustering algorithms, essential for discovering hidden structures in large volumes of unlabeled data.

In Chapter 15, you will learn advanced dimensionality reduction techniques using PCA and t-SNE, for visualization and optimization of complex data.

Chapter 16 presents effective methods for anomaly detection with Isolation Forest, enabling precise identification and handling of outliers.

In the final chapters, we further refine your practical skills: Chapter 17 focuses on creating automated Machine Learning pipelines, ensuring efficiency and scalability; Chapter 18 addresses advanced strategies for the safe and effective deployment of models in production environments, preparing you for real large-scale applications.

Chapter 19 teaches specialized techniques for dealing with imbalanced data, a common challenge in real projects, while Chapter 20 details the efficient integration of Scikit-Learn with other essential libraries such as Pandas and Matplotlib.

In Chapter 21, we present advanced concepts of Automation and AutoML, teaching practical tools to automate critical stages of the Machine Learning workflow. Then, in Chapter 22, you will master model interpretation and explainability through techniques such as SHAP and LIME, fundamental for strategic decision-making in sensitive scenarios.

Chapter 23 connects you to the Big Data universe, integrating Scikit-Learn with powerful tools like Spark and Dask, while Chapter 24 teaches how to apply advanced MLOps principles, including robust CI/CD strategies for models.

We conclude our journey in Chapter 25 with a chapter

dedicated to advanced model testing and debugging, ensuring maximum quality, performance, and efficiency in your practical implementations.

By following each chapter of this book, you will benefit from a clear and didactic structure, including detailed explanations, tested and real examples, solutions for common errors, recommended best practices, and concrete practical applications, ensuring progressive and results-focused learning.

By mastering the concepts and techniques presented in each chapter of this guide, you will be fully capable of creating robust, scalable, and effective Machine Learning solutions with Scikit-Learn, standing out as an indispensable professional in any Data Science team or project.

Welcome to the revolution of practical knowledge in Machine Learning with Scikit-Learn. This is the complete guide you need to transform theory into real and high-impact applications.

CHAPTER 1. WHAT IS SCIKIT-LEARN?

The universe of data science is growing at an accelerated pace, driven by the exponential increase in information generated by people and devices. With this advancement, the need for robust tools that enable accurate, fast, and practical analyses becomes imperative. In this scenario, Scikit-Learn stands out as an essential library for developing Machine Learning solutions in Python. This chapter provides a detailed introduction, exploring its history, features that differentiate it from other libraries, and detailing its modular architecture.

History and Evolution of Scikit-Learn

Scikit-Learn, also known as sklearn, is an open-source Machine Learning library written in Python. Its origin dates back to the Google Summer of Code project in 2007, developed by David Cournapeau as an extension of SciPy, a scientific library in Python. Initially, Scikit-Learn was simply called "scikits.learn," reflecting its nature as a modular complement to SciPy.

In 2010, after three years of community development and a significant expansion of features, the project gained independence as a standalone library, officially renamed Scikit-Learn. Since then, it has grown rapidly thanks to the active contribution of developers, data scientists, and academic researchers worldwide.

The initial philosophy of Scikit-Learn was to provide an easy-to-use, accessible, and consistent library. Today, it is widely adopted for its intuitive interface, robust documentation, and comprehensive variety of high-performance algorithms. Scikit-Learn has become an international reference in Machine Learning, widely used both in academia and by leading companies in the technology and data analysis sectors.

Difference Between Scikit-Learn and Other Machine Learning Libraries

Various Machine Learning libraries compete for space in the technical market, each with its own characteristics and specialties. Understanding the main differences between Scikit-Learn and other popular libraries helps you select the most appropriate tool for different application contexts.

Scikit-Learn vs. TensorFlow and PyTorch

TensorFlow and PyTorch are libraries specialized in deep learning. They are designed specifically to handle complex neural networks and require greater technical knowledge in configuring and developing models. Scikit-Learn, on the other hand, stands out for its ease of use, consistency in application, and quick implementation of traditional Machine Learning methods such as regression, classification, clustering, and data preprocessing.

While TensorFlow and PyTorch are ideal for complex problems involving large volumes of data and deep neural networks, Scikit-Learn offers simplicity for the rapid and efficient development of classic models and traditional solutions that do not exclusively depend on advanced neural network techniques.

Scikit-Learn vs. XGBoost, LightGBM, and CatBoost

Specialized libraries such as XGBoost, LightGBM, and CatBoost offer optimized and high-performance algorithms for tree-based ensemble methods such as Gradient Boosting. They often provide greater speed and efficiency in large datasets and competitive scenarios, such as Kaggle competitions.

Scikit-Learn also has robust ensemble algorithms, such as

Random Forest and Gradient Boosting, but generally offers less specialized and optimized implementations for very large or highly competitive tasks. However, it remains the best choice for an initial, more generalist approach or for projects requiring quick integration with other Python tools due to its standardized structure and clarity in practical application.

Scikit-Learn vs. Statsmodels

The Statsmodels library focuses on traditional statistics and econometrics, offering greater depth in detailed statistical analysis and hypothesis testing. Unlike Statsmodels, Scikit-Learn emphasizes a more direct approach to practical Machine Learning, with easy-to-use algorithms, pre-defined models, and simplified integration into automated pipelines.

Statsmodels is ideal for deep and detailed statistical analysis, while Scikit-Learn is preferable when the goal is the fast, clear, and direct construction of predictive models or classifiers applied to practical and market problems.

Component-Based Architecture and Its Importance

One of the most important factors that make Scikit-Learn popular among professionals and researchers is its modular component-based architecture. This architecture consists of standardized elements called estimators, transformers, and pipelines, organized into a consistent and easy-to-use interface.

Estimators

Estimators are objects capable of learning from the provided data. They receive input data, adjust their internal parameters, and return a trained model. Examples of estimators include linear regression models (LinearRegression), classifiers such as decision trees (DecisionTreeClassifier), and clusterers like KMeans (KMeans).

The standardization of these estimators in Scikit-Learn is especially important because it allows uniform use of different algorithms and techniques. All estimators follow a common interface with methods such as .fit() for training and .predict() to generate predictions.

For example, training an estimator model with Scikit-Learn involves just these simple steps:

python
```
from sklearn.linear_model import LinearRegression

model = LinearRegression()
model.fit(X_train, y_train)
predictions = model.predict(X_test)
```

This simple format is consistently repeated throughout the library.

Transformers

Transformers are objects that modify input data, preparing it to be used by estimators. They perform tasks such as normalization, scaling, encoding categorical variables, or dimensionality reduction.

Transformers share a standardized interface, using the .fit() method to learn necessary transformation parameters and .transform() to apply the transformation to the data:

python
```
from sklearn.preprocessing import StandardScaler

scaler = StandardScaler()
scaler.fit(X_train)
X_train_scaled = scaler.transform(X_train)
X_test_scaled = scaler.transform(X_test)
```

This interface pattern greatly facilitates the integration of transformers into preprocessing and modeling pipelines.

Pipelines

Pipelines are one of the greatest structural advantages of Scikit-Learn. They combine transformers and estimators into a logical sequence of steps that can be executed automatically. Pipelines ensure that the entire flow — from preprocessing to prediction — happens consistently and repeatably.

Practical example of a pipeline:

python
```
from sklearn.pipeline import Pipeline
from sklearn.preprocessing import StandardScaler
from sklearn.linear_model import LogisticRegression

pipeline = Pipeline([
    ('scaler', StandardScaler()),
    ('logistic_regression', LogisticRegression())
])

pipeline.fit(X_train, y_train)
predictions = pipeline.predict(X_test)
```

Pipelines not only simplify the code but also prevent common errors related to preprocessing consistency across different datasets (such as training and testing sets).

Common Errors and Recommended Solutions

Error: "ValueError: shapes not aligned"
This error occurs when the dimensions of the independent and dependent variables do not match.

Recommended Solution: Check the dimensions of the variables using .shape before fitting. Ensure that X (features) and y (target) have an equal number of samples (rows).

Error: "ModuleNotFoundError: No module named 'sklearn'"
Occurs when Scikit-Learn is not correctly installed in the Python environment.
Recommended Solution: Install the library using the command pip install scikit-learn. Then verify the installation using import sklearn in the Python environment.

Best Practices

- Always use pipelines to ensure consistency in processes.

- Use cross-validation to properly evaluate models before deploying them to production.

- Clearly document and organize each preprocessing step, using reproducible scripts.

Major companies such as Spotify, Airbnb, and Google apply Scikit-Learn daily in recommendation systems, customer segmentation, strategic forecasts, and fraud detection, highlighting its effectiveness and reliability in the market.

Scikit-Learn represents an indispensable tool in the arsenal of any modern data professional, combining clarity, efficiency, and practicality in a single platform. Deeply knowing its architecture, functioning, and real-world applications directly enhances your ability to deliver high-value and relevant results in the competitive data science and Machine Learning landscape.

CHAPTER 2. INSTALLING AND CONFIGURING THE ENVIRONMENT

To carry out effective Machine Learning projects, the first essential step is to properly configure your development environment. The goal is to ensure that all necessary tools are correctly installed and configured, allowing you to focus directly on model creation and analysis. This chapter will guide you through installing Python and Scikit-Learn, building an initial project, and explaining the typical structure used in real-world projects, ensuring a solid foundation for all future activities.

Installing Python and Scikit-Learn

Installing Python:

Python is the most popular and recommended language for data science and Machine Learning. To get started, visit the official website (python.org) and download the latest stable version. When running the installer, check the option Add Python to PATH to ensure you can easily access Python via the command line.

After installation, verify that everything was successful. Open your terminal (use cmd or Powershell on Windows, and Terminal on Mac and Linux) and run the following command:

bash

```
python --version
```

If the installation was successful, the installed Python version will appear, something like Python 3.12.0.

Installing Scikit-Learn with pip

With Python installed, the next step is to install Scikit-Learn. The quickest and simplest way is to use pip, Python's official package manager. Type the following command in the terminal:

bash
```
pip install scikit-learn
```

Additionally, we recommend installing other complementary libraries widely used in building Machine Learning models:

bash
```
pip install numpy pandas matplotlib seaborn
```

These libraries ensure complete support for data manipulation, visualization, and analysis.

Creating Virtual Environments (recommended)

A good practice is to use virtual environments to manage the dependencies of each project independently. This ensures that each project uses specific versions of the necessary libraries, avoiding future conflicts.

To create and activate a virtual environment, use:

bash
```
python -m venv projeto_ml
```

Activating on Windows:

bash
```
projeto_ml\Scripts\activate
```

Activating on Linux or Mac:

bash

```
source projeto_ml/bin/activate
```

Once activated, reinstall the libraries within this virtual environment using pip. This will guarantee greater control over your development environment.

Creating the First Machine Learning Project with Scikit-Learn

With the environment ready, it is time to create your first Machine Learning project using Scikit-Learn. This activity will help you understand the basic workflow and confirm that the previous installations were successful.

Create a folder for your project with an intuitive name, such as primeiro_projeto_ml, and inside it, create a file named modelo.py. In this file, implement the following basic script, which uses the Iris dataset included directly in Scikit-Learn:

python

```
# Importing essential libraries
from sklearn.datasets import load_iris
from sklearn.model_selection import train_test_split
from sklearn.linear_model import LogisticRegression
from sklearn.metrics import accuracy_score

# Loading the Iris dataset
iris = load_iris()
X = iris.data
y = iris.target

# Splitting data into training and testing sets (80% train, 20%
```

```
test)
X_train, X_test, y_train, y_test = train_test_split(X, y,
test_size=0.2, random_state=42)

# Creating and training the model
model = LogisticRegression(max_iter=200)
model.fit(X_train, y_train)

# Making predictions on the test data
predictions = model.predict(X_test)

# Evaluating model accuracy
accuracy = accuracy_score(y_test, predictions)
print(f"Model accuracy: {accuracy * 100:.2f}%")
```

Explaining the Code Step by Step

- We import essential libraries, including datasets and specific functions from Scikit-Learn.

- The Iris dataset contains data about three different species of the Iris flower, widely used as an initial example in Machine Learning.

- train_test_split automatically splits the dataset into training and testing parts.

- LogisticRegression is a classic model used for categorical data classification.

- The .fit() method trains the model on the training data.

- The .predict() method makes predictions based on the trained model.

- accuracy_score evaluates the accuracy of predictions by comparing them to the real values.

Run the code through the command in the terminal:

bash

```
python modelo.py
```

The result will be the model's accuracy, confirming that all previous steps were performed correctly.

Basic Structure of Scikit-Learn Projects

An organized structure is essential for managing projects efficiently and professionally. A typical recommended structure would resemble the following pattern:

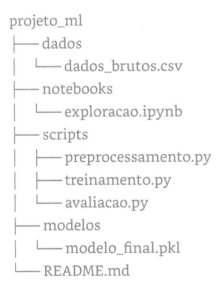

```
projeto_ml
├── dados
│   └── dados_brutos.csv
├── notebooks
│   └── exploracao.ipynb
├── scripts
│   ├── preprocessamento.py
│   ├── treinamento.py
│   └── avaliacao.py
├── modelos
│   └── modelo_final.pkl
└── README.md
```

- The dados folder stores used and manipulated datasets.

- notebooks contains exploratory analyses, generally done with Jupyter Notebook.

- The scripts folder centralizes all Python scripts for the project, organized by workflow stage.

- modelos stores trained and serialized models for later use.

- The README.md file provides important information and clear instructions for anyone using or collaborating on the project.

Testing the Installation with Basic Commands

In addition to the code already created, a quick way to test if everything is correctly configured is to directly execute commands in Python's interactive terminal. Open the Python terminal by typing in the operating system terminal:

bash

```
python
```

Then type the following commands to validate the installations:

python

```
import sklearn
import numpy
import pandas
print("Libraries installed successfully!")
```

If no error message appears, all libraries are correctly installed and ready for use.

Common Errors and Recommended Solutions

Error: Command 'python' not found

This error indicates that Python is not properly added to the system PATH.

Recommended Solution: Reinstall Python, ensuring to check the "Add Python to PATH" option during installation. Restart the terminal after installation.

Error: ModuleNotFoundError: No module named 'sklearn'
This error occurs when Scikit-Learn is not installed in the active Python environment.
Recommended Solution: Run pip install scikit-learn in the terminal with the virtual environment activated. Then confirm with the pip list command.

Error: ValueError or error related to incompatible shapes when executing code
This error often occurs when the number of samples does not match between independent and dependent variables.
Recommended Solution: Use the .shape method from NumPy or Pandas to check the dimensions of all variables before performing training or predictions.

Best Practices and Real Applications

- Always use virtual environments to manage project-specific dependencies, avoiding conflicts between libraries.

- Use version control (such as Git) to track the history of changes in the project, especially when working in teams or on complex projects.

- Standardize your folder structure across all projects, making organization and collaboration easier.

- Automate repetitive steps using reusable scripts whenever possible.

- Regularly validate models using techniques like cross-validation to ensure robust and reliable results.

Recognized companies such as Spotify, Netflix, and Amazon routinely use Scikit-Learn as part of their Machine Learning technical infrastructure to recommend content, optimize internal operations, and predict strategic market trends, demonstrating its real value and applicability in highly demanding scenarios.

Proper installation and configuration of the environment for projects with Python and Scikit-Learn are fundamental to ensure efficiency, consistency, and productivity at all subsequent stages of Machine Learning. With this structured and functional environment, you are fully prepared to deeply explore the potential of data, build advanced models, and generate real and impactful results with confidence and speed.

CHAPTER 3. STRUCTURE AND FUNDAMENTAL CONCEPTS

When dealing with Machine Learning using Scikit-Learn, deeply understanding its basic structure and fundamental concepts becomes indispensable. Understanding how this library is built facilitates its intuitive use, increases productivity, and ensures the technical quality of the projects developed.

Scikit-Learn stands out for the clarity of its component-based architecture, its logical organization, and ease of expansion and integration with other data science tools. In this context, we will thoroughly address the fundamental components, the role of structural directives and attributes, and how Python acts as a key language to fully leverage the library's potential.

Components, Templates, and Metadata

Scikit-Learn's architecture is based on three essential types of objects: estimators, transformers, and predictors. These components have standardized behavior, ensuring consistency when using different algorithms or techniques available in the library.

Estimators

Estimators are central objects in Scikit-Learn. They learn patterns directly from data. Estimators always implement two mandatory methods: .fit() and .predict() (or .transform(), depending on the type). The .fit() method trains the model, learning the characteristics of the dataset. The .predict() method makes predictions using the knowledge acquired during training.

python

```
from sklearn.linear_model import LinearRegression

# Creating the LinearRegression estimator
estimator = LinearRegression()

# Fitting the data (training the model)
estimator.fit(X_train, y_train)

# Making predictions
predictions = estimator.predict(X_test)
```

In the code above, LinearRegression is an estimator that learns the relationship between independent variables and a dependent variable, enabling accurate predictions.

Transformers

Transformers are responsible for altering input data, usually to improve or prepare it for estimators. They implement two main methods: .fit() to learn parameters and .transform() to apply transformations. The primary applications are data cleaning, normalization, scaling, and encoding.

python

```
from sklearn.preprocessing import StandardScaler

# Creating the StandardScaler transformer
transformer = StandardScaler()

# Learning the scale of training data
transformer.fit(X_train)

# Applying transformation
```

```
X_train_scaled = transformer.transform(X_train)
X_test_scaled = transformer.transform(X_test)
```

In the case above, StandardScaler normalizes the data so that each feature has zero mean and unit variance, ensuring that the model receives uniform data for learning.

Predictors

Predictors are specific types of estimators that generate predictions based on the trained model. A predictor is always the result of an estimator that has already been trained with the .fit() method. The main difference is its practical use: after training, it is directly applied to generate results.

Each of these objects (estimators, transformers, and predictors) can be combined into pipelines that automate complex steps with clarity and ease. These components are modular, allowing efficient reuse and rapid adaptation according to the project's technical needs.

Structural Directives and Attributes

Scikit-Learn has clear structural directives and attributes to ensure proper functioning of models and transformations. They are simple yet essential conventions that determine how data is handled within objects.

fit() Method
This mandatory method initializes training, whether in estimators or transformers. When calling .fit(), the model analyzes and learns internal information about the provided data.

python
```
model.fit(X, y)
```

predict() Method
Available in trained estimators, .predict() generates predictions

based on the training performed by .fit().

python
prediction = model.predict(X_new)

transform() Method
Implemented in transformers, .transform() is used to make changes to the data (e.g., scaling, encoding) after adjustment with .fit().

python
X_transformed = transformer.transform(X)

These methods ensure consistency and allow different models and transformers to be used with the same logic and simplicity.

Introduction to Python and Its Role in Scikit-Learn

Python is an interpreted, dynamic, versatile, and highly productive language widely used in data science. The popularity of Python in this field stems from its simple syntax, large community, vast amount of specialized libraries, and extensive support for integrations with other tools and systems.

In the specific context of Scikit-Learn, Python acts as the base language and direct interface to access all library features. Integration with other scientific libraries in Python — NumPy, Pandas, Matplotlib, and Seaborn — allows for a complete and integrated workflow for Machine Learning.

Python's role is central because it offers a clean and clear syntax, allowing professionals, even those with little experience, to quickly implement complex solutions. Additionally, Python enables the development of robust applications, ranging from quick analyses to production systems.

Basic example clearly demonstrating Python's role integrated with Scikit-Learn:

python

```python
# Essential imports
import numpy as np
import pandas as pd
from sklearn.model_selection import train_test_split
from sklearn.ensemble import RandomForestClassifier
from sklearn.metrics import accuracy_score

# Fictional data for demonstration
data = pd.DataFrame({
    'age': [25, 30, 45, 35, 22, 41],
    'salary': [5000, 6000, 8000, 6500, 4500, 8500],
    'purchased': [0, 1, 1, 0, 0, 1]
})

# Separating independent and dependent variables
X = data[['age', 'salary']]
y = data['purchased']

# Splitting into training and testing sets
X_train, X_test, y_train, y_test = train_test_split(X, y,
test_size=0.3, random_state=42)

# Random Forest model
model_rf = RandomForestClassifier(n_estimators=100)

# Training the model
model_rf.fit(X_train, y_train)

# Prediction
y_pred = model_rf.predict(X_test)

# Evaluation
```

```
accuracy = accuracy_score(y_test, y_pred)
print(f"Model accuracy: {accuracy:.2f}")
```

The example above demonstrates how Python facilitates the integration, manipulation, and execution of Scikit-Learn, ensuring that each step of the process is clear, precise, and intuitive.

Common Errors and Recommended Solutions

Error: AttributeError: 'transform' not found
This error indicates an attempt to use .transform() on estimators that do not have this functionality.
Recommended Solution: Always confirm the object type. Only transformers have the .transform() method. In predictive estimators, use .predict().

Error: NotFittedError: Instance not fitted yet
This error occurs when calling .predict() or .transform() before training with .fit().
Recommended Solution: Always perform training first with .fit() before generating predictions or transformations. Ensure that the execution order is clear: first fit, then use the model.

Best Practices and Real Applications

- Always use pipelines to standardize and automate your Machine Learning workflow, ensuring quality and ease of maintenance.

- Clearly document the steps taken in each transformation and estimation, facilitating collaboration and later review.

- Regularly and thoroughly test models, using techniques like cross-validation.

- Organize and standardize code through reusable functions and classes, ensuring efficiency and reducing errors.

Global organizations, such as banks, e-commerce companies, and major academic institutions, adopt Scikit-Learn in critical processes. Examples include credit classification in banks, recommendation systems on digital platforms, and precise medical predictions in specialized hospitals, proving its versatility and effectiveness.

A deep understanding of Scikit-Learn's structure and fundamental concepts provides a solid foundation for carrying out efficient Machine Learning projects. By mastering components, structural directives, and the central role of Python in the library, you ensure greater productivity, technical accuracy, and confidence in all solutions developed, being fully prepared to tackle real and complex challenges with technical clarity and effectiveness.

CHAPTER 4. WORKING WITH ESTIMATORS

Mastering the concept of estimators is a decisive step toward building efficient solutions with Scikit-Learn. An estimator, in the clearest and most objective definition, is an object that learns from provided data and generates predictions or insights based on that learning. Every Machine Learning model in Scikit-Learn is implemented as an estimator, and all follow a uniform structure, allowing easy learning, usage, and maintenance. A clear understanding of how to correctly work with these estimators enables you to extract valuable and accurate results from data.

Components, Templates, and Metadata

Estimators are essential and structuring elements in Scikit-Learn. They have three basic characteristics that define their operation: consistency, modularity, and standardization.

Each estimator offers a uniform interface that includes specific methods such as .fit(), .predict(), .transform(), and .score(). This standardization is fundamental to ensure that different models and techniques can be applied quickly and consistently, simplifying professionals' work and reducing the possibility of technical errors.

.fit() Method

The .fit() method is the central component of all estimators in Scikit-Learn. When executed, it allows the estimator to learn the model's specific parameters directly from the provided data.

python

```
from sklearn.linear_model import LogisticRegression

# Training data
X_train = [[0, 0], [1, 1], [2, 2], [3, 3]]
y_train = [0, 0, 1, 1]

# Creating and training the model
model = LogisticRegression()
model.fit(X_train, y_train)
```

In this code, the LogisticRegression estimator is trained with a simple dataset. The .fit() method allows the model to adjust its internal parameters to understand the existing relationship between variables.

.predict() Method

After the training stage, the .predict() method is used to make predictions with new data.

python

```
# New data for prediction
X_new = [[1.5, 1.5], [0.5, 0.5]]

# Making predictions
predictions = model.predict(X_new)
print(predictions)
```

By using .predict(), the already trained estimator generates predictions directly, allowing you to make quick decisions based on the obtained results.

.transform() Method

Some estimators have the specific function of transforming data. These are called transformers and differ from predictors because they do not return predictions but new data formats.

python
```
from sklearn.preprocessing import MinMaxScaler

# Original data
X = [[10, 100], [20, 200], [30, 300]]

# Scaling data
scaler = MinMaxScaler()
X_scaled = scaler.fit_transform(X)
print(X_scaled)
```

In this code, the MinMaxScaler transformer applies a transformation that scales the data between a specific range (usually between 0 and 1), ensuring that the data is at the ideal scale for subsequent estimators.

.score() Method

The .score() method provides a simple and quick way to evaluate the performance of the trained model using a validation or test dataset.

python
```
# Evaluating model performance
accuracy = model.score(X_train, y_train)
print(f"Model accuracy: {accuracy:.2f}")
```

This function facilitates quick and direct evaluations of the results achieved by the trained model.

Structural Directives and Attributes

Scikit-Learn has specific structural directives for estimators. These directives ensure standardized and consistent behavior of models.

- Every estimator must be instantiated before use, meaning a variable representing the chosen model must be created.

- Before making predictions, the estimator must be trained with .fit().

- Internal attributes of each estimator (for example, .coef_ for linear regression coefficients or .feature_importances_ for feature importance in decision trees) become available after the execution of the .fit() method.

Practical example demonstrating internal attributes after training:

python

```
from sklearn.linear_model import LinearRegression

# Training data
X = [[1], [2], [3], [4]]
y = [2, 4, 6, 8]

# Model and training
model = LinearRegression()
model.fit(X, y)

# Displaying internal attributes (coefficients)
print(model.coef_)
print(model.intercept_)
```

These attributes provide direct insights into how the model learned the relationship between the analyzed variables.

Introduction to Scikit-Learn

Estimators and Basic Algorithms

Scikit-Learn provides a wide range of estimators designed for different types of problems, whether classification, regression, clustering, or dimensionality reduction.

Estimators for Classification

Classification consists of identifying which category an observation belongs to. Common examples of classifier estimators are:

- LogisticRegression: Mainly used for binary or simple multiclass problems.

- DecisionTreeClassifier: Efficient for interpreting and visualizing decisions.

- RandomForestClassifier: Powerful in avoiding overfitting and useful for large and complex datasets.

Estimators for Regression

Regression predicts continuous numerical values. Popular examples:

- LinearRegression: Classic estimator for linear relationships.

- DecisionTreeRegressor: Great for nonlinear models, offering interpretability.

- RandomForestRegressor: Good performance in complex scenarios with a lot of data.

Estimators for Clustering

Estimators group unlabeled data into similar sets, automatically identifying patterns or segments. Some examples are:

- KMeans: Creates clusters by identifying group centers.

- DBSCAN: Groups data based on density, excellent for irregularly shaped data.

Estimators for Dimensionality Reduction

These estimators simplify complex data while retaining essential information. Important examples are:

- PCA: Reduces dimensionality by creating new variables that preserve the greatest possible variance.

- t-SNE: Widely used for visualization in two or three dimensions.

Common Errors and Recommended Solutions

Error: ValueError "shapes (x,y) and (a,b) not aligned"

This error occurs due to the mismatch of variable dimensions. Recommended Solution: Always use .shape from NumPy to check dimensions before performing operations:

```python
print(X_train.shape)
print(y_train.shape)
```

Error: AttributeError "'Model' object has no attribute 'predict'"
This error indicates an attempt to use .predict() on a transformer.
Recommended Solution: Check the documentation of the estimator used and ensure it is a trained predictor with .fit()

before calling .predict().

Error: NotFittedError "This estimator instance is not fitted yet."
Means an attempt to predict before training the model.
Recommended Solution: Always use .fit() before .predict() to
ensure prior learning.

Best Practices and Real Applications

- Use pipelines to manage multiple estimators sequentially, automating processes and preventing common errors.

- Choose appropriate estimators for the specific type of problem. For simple problems, use linear models as a first approach; for complex problems, prefer RandomForest or XGBoost.

- Regularly validate with cross-validation to confirm results and model stability.

- Use properly tuned hyperparameters to ensure models are neither overfitting nor underfitting.

Major tech companies use Scikit-Learn estimators in processes such as fraud detection, price forecasting, and personalized content recommendation, demonstrating real-world applicability and proven technical effectiveness.

Deep knowledge of estimators ensures high technical productivity and real capability to solve complex data problems. By understanding how to use them, which methods and attributes are most effective, you will be able to quickly create accurate and reliable models, achieving consistent and effective results capable of generating real and significant impact in the Machine Learning projects you develop.

CHAPTER 5. DATA PREPROCESSING

Data preprocessing is a crucial step in any Machine Learning project. Often, the quality of results depends directly on the efficiency and accuracy of the techniques applied during this process. Raw data often contains noise, inconsistent values, missing information, and varying scales that, if not properly handled, negatively impact the performance of predictive models.

Scikit-Learn provides a robust set of tools specifically designed to simplify and optimize data preprocessing. These tools follow a standardized, intuitive, and easy-to-apply structure, allowing you to create efficient pipelines with clarity and speed.

Components, Templates, and Metadata

The Scikit-Learn library uses well-defined components divided into transformers and estimators. In the specific context of data preprocessing, transformers are the most relevant components, as they allow altering, adjusting, and preparing the data for the subsequent steps of machine learning.

Each transformer follows a structure clearly defined by the following main methods:

- .fit(): learns parameters directly from the data;

- .transform(): applies transformations to the data based on the learned parameters;

- .fit_transform(): combines the two steps above for greater convenience and clarity in the code.

These methods provide a consistent and standardized interface for different types of transformations, ensuring that you can use them precisely and quickly in various contexts.

Fundamental Transformers in Preprocessing

Among the most used transformers, the highlights are:

- StandardScaler: standardizes data to have zero mean and unit standard deviation;

- MinMaxScaler: normalizes data within defined intervals, usually from 0 to 1;

- RobustScaler: used for data with significant presence of outliers;

- SimpleImputer: handles missing values, replacing them with defined values such as mean or median;

- OneHotEncoder: encodes categorical variables into binary numerical representations;

- OrdinalEncoder: assigns ordered numerical values to categorical variables;

- PolynomialFeatures: generates polynomial combinations and interactions between variables, enriching the feature space.

Each of these components is modular and can be easily combined into pipelines, ensuring efficient automation and technical quality during preprocessing.

Structural Directives and Attributes

When working with preprocessing transformers in Scikit-Learn, it is essential to clearly understand the structural directives and standard attributes.

Essential Structural Directives

- All transformers must be instantiated before use.

- The .fit() method always precedes the .transform() method, as the transformation needs previously learned parameters.

- The .fit_transform() method offers convenience by combining fitting and transformation into a single step.

Practical example of the structural directives with StandardScaler:

python
```
from sklearn.preprocessing import StandardScaler

# Original data
X = [[100, 0.001], [8, 0.05], [50, 0.005]]

# Instantiating the transformer
scaler = StandardScaler()

# Learning parameters from the data and applying
transformation
X_scaled = scaler.fit_transform(X)

print(X_scaled)
```

In the code above, StandardScaler calculates the mean and

standard deviation for each feature during .fit() and uses these values in the .transform() step to standardize the data, ensuring zero mean and unit variance.

Introduction to Preprocessing

Techniques with Scikit-Learn

Scikit-Learn offers practical techniques to preprocess data with high efficiency. Here are some of the most frequently applied techniques and how you can use them with clarity and precision.

Handling Missing Values

Missing values directly compromise model learning quality. A robust and simple technique to handle them is using SimpleImputer.

```python
from sklearn.impute import SimpleImputer
import numpy as np

X = [[np.nan, 2], [6, np.nan], [7, 6]]

# Replacing missing values with column means
imputer = SimpleImputer(strategy='mean')
X_filled = imputer.fit_transform(X)

print(X_filled)
```

In this code, missing values are automatically filled with the mean of each column, eliminating inconsistencies from the data.

Encoding Categorical Variables

Non-numeric categorical variables need to be converted before model training. An efficient technique is OneHotEncoder.

python

```
from sklearn.preprocessing import OneHotEncoder

categorical_data = [['Brazil'], ['Chile'], ['Argentina'], ['Brazil']]

encoder = OneHotEncoder(sparse=False)
encoded_categories = encoder.fit_transform(categorical_data)

print(encoded_categories)
```

In this procedure, categories are converted into clear binary numerical representations, facilitating correct model interpretation.

Scaling and Normalization

Scaling ensures that variables are within the same range or scale. Using MinMaxScaler is effective in ensuring data consistency.

python

```
from sklearn.preprocessing import MinMaxScaler

data = [[20, 5000], [25, 5500], [30, 6000]]

scaler = MinMaxScaler()
scaled_data = scaler.fit_transform(data)

print(scaled_data)
```

Here, all data is resized to a standard range (0-1), ensuring uniformity and stability in model training.

Removing Outliers

Outliers are extreme values that directly impact model quality.

Using RobustScaler ensures stability against these values.

python

```
from sklearn.preprocessing import RobustScaler

data_with_outliers = [[1], [2], [5], [100]]

robust_scaler = RobustScaler()
robust_data = robust_scaler.fit_transform(data_with_outliers)

print(robust_data)
```

RobustScaler applies a transformation based on medians, significantly minimizing the influence of outliers on the data.

Common Errors and Recommended Solutions

Error: "Input contains NaN"
Indicates the presence of missing values when applying algorithms directly.
Recommended Solution: Always use imputation techniques, such as SimpleImputer, before any model training.

Error: "ValueError: could not convert string to float"
Occurs when trying to use unconverted categorical data.
Recommended Solution: Always use OneHotEncoder or OrdinalEncoder to convert categorical data before using them in model training.

Error: "NotFittedError: Instance not fitted yet"
Occurs when trying to transform data before fitting the transformer with .fit().
Recommended Solution: Always execute .fit() before calling .transform(). For initial steps, use .fit_transform() for greater clarity.

Best Practices and Real Applications

- Always visually validate the results of transformations using graphs or histograms to verify effectiveness.

- Create pipelines to automate and ensure consistent preprocessing for training, testing, and production data.

- Always record the exact sequence of transformations applied, ensuring reproducibility and transparency of the process.

- Use robust transformations on sensitive or critical data, such as RobustScaler for financial data.

Major organizations, such as financial institutions and e-commerce companies, rigorously apply preprocessing techniques with Scikit-Learn to ensure reliable and stable predictions in scenarios such as credit analysis, personalized recommendations, and fraud detection.

The quality of the data is fundamental to obtaining robust and efficient Machine Learning models. By mastering the preprocessing techniques provided by Scikit-Learn, you will ensure greater precision, clarity, and effectiveness in model generation. With these practices, you will be fully capable of transforming raw data into real insights and strategic decisions, ensuring trust and superior results in all your data projects.

CHAPTER 6. FEATURE ENGINEERING WITH SCIKIT-LEARN

The effectiveness of Machine Learning models is directly related to the quality of the variables or attributes used in their training. Often, even sophisticated algorithms fail to generate consistent results when the characteristics of the data have not been correctly defined, selected, or transformed. To address this issue, feature engineering becomes a crucial step in any data science project.

Feature Engineering is the process of selecting, creating, and transforming original variables, directly improving the predictive capability of models. Scikit-Learn provides a wide range of tools that make this step intuitive, practical, and efficient, ensuring precision, speed, and clarity in the process of creating and selecting quality features.

Components, Templates, and Metadata

Scikit-Learn's modular structure allows you to create and manipulate features in an organized and efficient way through standardized components. In this step, the main components are the specific transformers for Feature Engineering. They always follow the same interface with standard methods, facilitating their implementation and use.

Fundamental Transformers in Feature Engineering

Some of the essential transformers from Scikit-Learn for feature engineering include:

- PolynomialFeatures: generates new attributes by combining existing variables at different degrees.

- OneHotEncoder: transforms categorical variables into numerical ones, facilitating interpretation by algorithms.

- OrdinalEncoder: assigns sequential numerical values to categories, preserving the natural order of information.

- KBinsDiscretizer: converts continuous variables into discrete categories, simplifying data interpretation by models.

Each component uses standard methods such as .fit(), .transform(), and .fit_transform(), allowing easy integration into structured pipelines. This uniformity ensures greater productivity and technical precision in feature creation and selection.

Structural Directives and Attributes

To ensure efficiency and clarity in using Feature Engineering components, Scikit-Learn establishes fundamental structural directives that must be followed at every step of the process:

- All transformers must be instantiated before use.

- Each transformer must first be fitted to the data with .fit() before applying transformations with .transform().

- Use the .fit_transform() method to simplify and speed up processes whenever applicable.

Example of structural directives using the PolynomialFeatures transformer:

python

```
from sklearn.preprocessing import PolynomialFeatures
import numpy as np

# Original data
X = np.array([[2, 3],
              [4, 5],
              [6, 7]])

# Creating polynomial attributes (degree 2)
poly = PolynomialFeatures(degree=2, include_bias=False)

# Learning and transforming the data
X_poly = poly.fit_transform(X)

print(X_poly)
```

The PolynomialFeatures transformer creates new attributes resulting from interactions between existing variables, allowing models to capture more complex and refined relationships in the data.

Introduction to Preprocessing

Techniques with Scikit-Learn

In the context of Feature Engineering, advanced techniques to enhance and enrich the original data base are especially highlighted. Among the main ones are automatic feature creation, encoding categorical variables, and advanced automatic feature selection techniques.

Creating Polynomial Features (PolynomialFeatures)

The polynomial features technique allows generating new variables by combining existing attributes. This technique is particularly effective when the relationship between variables and the final outcome is not linear, enabling better model performance.

Detailed code explaining the use of PolynomialFeatures:

python

```
from sklearn.preprocessing import PolynomialFeatures
import numpy as np

# Original data (features)
X = np.array([[3], [5], [7]])

# Generating new polynomial attributes (degree 2)
poly = PolynomialFeatures(degree=2, include_bias=False)
X_poly = poly.fit_transform(X)

print("Original attributes:\n", X)
print("New polynomial attributes:\n", X_poly)
```

The result is new attributes derived from the original variables, allowing the model to capture complex patterns not evident in the initial data analysis.

Encoding Categorical Variables

Scikit-Learn offers two essential transformers for encoding categorical variables: OneHotEncoder and OrdinalEncoder.

- OneHotEncoder transforms categories into binary vectors, ideal for nominal data without a specific order.

- OrdinalEncoder assigns integer numbers to each category, maintaining a natural order or hierarchy if present.

Detailed application code with OneHotEncoder:

python

```
from sklearn.preprocessing import OneHotEncoder
```

```
import numpy as np

# Original categorical variables
X_categorical = np.array([['Brazil'], ['Germany'], ['Brazil'],
['Argentina']])

# OneHotEncoder for encoding
encoder = OneHotEncoder(sparse=False)
X_encoded = encoder.fit_transform(X_categorical)

print(X_encoded)
```

Each category is transformed into a unique binary representation. This process allows Machine Learning algorithms to clearly interpret categorical variables, ensuring optimal performance in complex problems.

Automatic Feature Selection

Selecting the correct attributes is also crucial. Scikit-Learn offers SelectKBest, an efficient method to automatically select the best features based on statistical relevance to the target.

Detailed example using SelectKBest:

python
```
from sklearn.feature_selection import SelectKBest, chi2
import numpy as np

# Original data
X = np.array([[10, 0, 5, 6],
        [8, 0, 6, 9],
        [3, 8, 2, 1],
        [4, 1, 3, 7]])

# Target variable
```

```
y = np.array([1, 0, 0, 1])

# Selecting the two best features
selector = SelectKBest(score_func=chi2, k=2)
X_selected = selector.fit_transform(X, y)

print(X_selected)
```

Here, the two features with the best correlation with the target variable are automatically chosen, reducing model complexity and increasing performance.

Common Errors and Recommended Solutions

Error: ValueError with PolynomialFeatures due to inconsistent dimensions
This error occurs when data passed to PolynomialFeatures does not have the correct shape (it must always be two-dimensional). Recommended Solution: Confirm the correct data shape using .reshape(-1, 1) for one-dimensional vectors before using PolynomialFeatures.

python
```
X = np.array([2, 4, 6]).reshape(-1, 1)
```

Error: Categorical data not recognized by OneHotEncoder
Occurs when categorical data is not properly formatted before encoding.
Recommended Solution: Always ensure that categorical variables are in two-dimensional array format before the encoder.

python

```
X_categorical = np.array(['Brazil', 'Argentina']).reshape(-1,1)
```

Best Practices and Real Applications

- Use Pipeline to clearly automate each step of Feature Engineering, ensuring reproducibility and consistency.

- Always evaluate the impact of creating new features on overall model performance.

- Prioritize simple and efficient techniques initially, advancing to more complex methods only after a careful analysis of the impact on results.

Global organizations, especially technology companies and financial institutions, rigorously use these techniques to generate robust and efficient models in areas such as demand forecasting, credit risk classification, and personalized recommendation systems.

Mastering Feature Engineering with Scikit-Learn allows you to transform ordinary data into relevant and strategic information, boosting the accuracy and effectiveness of Machine Learning models.

CHAPTER 7. REGRESSION MODELS

Regression is one of the most important and widely used techniques in Machine Learning. It allows professionals to make accurate numerical predictions, identifying relationships and patterns in data that can be translated into concrete values. From financial projections to real-time estimates of demands or consumptions, regression is fundamental for assertive and strategic decision-making.

Scikit-Learn offers a robust and varied set of models for regression, covering from simple and easy-to-understand methods to sophisticated algorithms capable of extracting complex patterns from data.

Components, Templates, and Metadata

To properly understand the practical application of regression models in Scikit-Learn, it is necessary to clearly know its modular and standardized structure. These models, called estimators in Scikit-Learn, always follow a consistent and predictable structure, facilitating adoption and increasing operational efficiency during development.

All estimators, including regression models, have fundamental methods:

- .fit(): trains the model with input data;

- .predict(): generates predictions after training;

- .score(): quickly evaluates performance with test data.

This uniformity allows professionals to use different algorithms easily, maintaining a coherent flow across different contexts.

Structural Directives and Attributes

Scikit-Learn regression models follow a specific pattern of creation, adjustment, and use. Every regression model must be instantiated before being used. After that, you must always fit it to the data using the .fit() method before making predictions with .predict().

Additionally, each estimator has important internal attributes after training, such as:

- .coef_: model coefficients, indicating the strength and direction of the variables.

- .intercept_: the point where the line crosses the vertical axis, in the case of linear models.

These attributes provide a clear view of the relationship between variables and allow for quick interpretation of the model.

python
```
from sklearn.linear_model import LinearRegression
import numpy as np

X = np.array([[1], [2], [3], [4]])
y = np.array([3, 5, 7, 9])

model = LinearRegression()
model.fit(X, y)

# Coefficients learned by the model
```

```python
print("Coefficient:", model.coef_)
print("Intercept:", model.intercept_)
```

Here, LinearRegression() trains a simple model that directly relates two variables. The obtained coefficient (model.coef_) shows how much the dependent variable varies on average for each unit of the independent variable.

Introduction to Linear and

Nonlinear Regression Models

Regression is essentially divided into two major groups: linear and nonlinear. Each has its own characteristics, advantages, and limitations, being applicable in different technical contexts.

Simple Linear Regression

Simple linear regression predicts a dependent variable using only one independent variable. Its simplicity is its greatest asset, as it allows quick interpretation and direct application.

Detailed practical code:

python
```python
from sklearn.linear_model import LinearRegression
import numpy as np

# Simplified data
X = np.array([[5], [7], [9], [11]])
y = np.array([12, 15, 18, 21])

# Creating and fitting the linear model
linear_model = LinearRegression()
linear_model.fit(X, y)

# Making a prediction for a new value
prediction = linear_model.predict([[13]])
```

```
print("Predicted value:", prediction)
```

In this case, the model learns a direct relationship between X and y. This facilitates quick and assertive predictions based on clear and simple linear relationships.

Multiple Linear Regression

Multiple linear regression expands simple regression by using more independent variables. It captures simultaneous relationships between several features and the expected outcome.

python
```
X = np.array([[1, 2], [2, 3], [3, 5], [4, 7]])
y = np.array([10, 13, 20, 25])

multi_model = LinearRegression()
multi_model = multi_model.fit(X, y)

print("Coefficients:", multi_model.coef_)
print("Intercept:", multi_model.intercept_)
```

In the example above, additional variables allow for greater precision in prediction, identifying multiple simultaneous influences.

Nonlinear Regression Models

Many real-world problems cannot be adequately described by linear relationships. Scikit-Learn offers powerful nonlinear regression algorithms, especially useful for complex problems.

Detailed example with DecisionTreeRegressor (nonlinear):

python
```
from sklearn.tree import DecisionTreeRegressor
```

```python
X = np.array([[1], [3], [5], [7]])
y = np.array([1, 9, 25, 49])

nonlinear_model = DecisionTreeRegressor()
nonlinear_model.fit(X, y)

prediction = nonlinear_model.predict([[5]])
print("Prediction for value 5:", prediction)
```

This model is capable of learning nonlinear patterns in the data, allowing the capture of complex and non-evident relationships, ensuring precise predictions in more complex scenarios.

Random Forest and Advanced Regression

Random Forest is a model based on multiple decision trees, ideal for robust and more complex regressions. It is widely used in situations where data contains significant noise or complex nonlinear patterns.

python
```python
from sklearn.ensemble import RandomForestRegressor

X = [[10], [20], [30], [40], [50]]
y = [100, 200, 300, 400, 500]

rf_model = RandomForestRegressor(n_estimators=100)
rf_model.fit(X, y)

result = rf_model.predict([[25]])
print("Prediction with Random Forest:", result)
```

This method is robust, adaptable, and often produces accurate results even in complex and highly noisy situations.

Common Errors and Recommended Solutions

Error: "ValueError: Shapes not aligned"
This error often arises when using multiple regression with incompatible data dimensions.
Recommended Solution: Carefully check the dimensions of the variables using .shape. Ensure that the number of observations in the independent and dependent variables is the same.

Error: "NotFittedError: Estimator not fitted yet"
Occurs when trying to use .predict() before the .fit() method.
Recommended Solution: Always run the .fit() method first before making predictions with .predict().

Error: "AttributeError: object has no attribute 'coef_'"
Occurs when trying to access attributes before the model is fitted.
Recommended Solution: Always train the model before accessing internal attributes such as .coef_ or .intercept_.

Best Practices and Real Applications

- Use cross-validation to rigorously evaluate the performance of regression models, confirming result stability.

- Visually evaluate regression results through clear and intuitive graphs, facilitating quick interpretation of results.

- Prefer starting with simple linear models, migrating to nonlinear regression only when strictly necessary.

- Clearly document all transformation and regression

steps, allowing for efficient technical reviews and future maintenance.

Real applications include sales forecasting, service demand prediction, dynamic pricing, financial analysis, and other critical situations in modern organizations.

Leading companies use Scikit-Learn regression models in strategic financial decisions, ensuring operational effectiveness and technical assertiveness in highly competitive contexts.

With a clear mastery of regression models, you will have essential technical tools to transform large volumes of data into practical insights, robust predictions, and effective strategic decisions. The knowledge presented provides the entire technical foundation to ensure that you achieve precise, interpretable, and consistent models, creating real and impactful value in all your professional data science projects.

CHAPTER 8. CLASSIFICATION MODELS

Classification is one of the pillars of Machine Learning, enabling the efficient categorization of data into different classes. Classification applications include everything from visual pattern recognition to financial fraud detection. In Scikit-Learn, classification models offer robust solutions to transform large volumes of data into precise and actionable predictions.

With a standardized and highly modular interface, classifiers in Scikit-Learn ensure ease of use and integration with automated pipelines. Understanding their characteristics and functionality allows you to select the ideal model for each situation, ensuring efficiency and performance.

Components, Templates, and Metadata

Classification models in Scikit-Learn are built on three fundamental principles: consistency, modularity, and standardization. Each classifier follows a well-defined logical flow, ensuring predictability and efficiency in development.

All classifiers share a common structure:

- .fit(X, y): fits the model to the provided data.

- .predict(new_X): generates predictions based on the learned patterns.

- .score(X_test, y_test): evaluates the model's accuracy.

Additionally, each model may contain specific attributes that store important information after training, such as:

- .coef_: internal model coefficients for linear classifiers.

- .feature_importances_: relative importance of each feature in tree-based models.

Such modular structure facilitates the exchange and experimentation among different classifiers without the need for major changes in the code.

Structural Directives and Attributes

The implementation of classifiers in Scikit-Learn follows well-defined structural rules:

- Every model must be instantiated before being trained.

- The .fit() method must always be executed before .predict().

- Model validation should be done with appropriate metrics, such as accuracy, precision, and recall.

Scikit-Learn provides specific metrics for classifier evaluation, such as classification_report() and confusion_matrix(), which are essential for detailed performance analysis.

Practical example of instantiation, training, and evaluation:

python
```
from sklearn.model_selection import train_test_split
from sklearn.datasets import load_wine
from sklearn.ensemble import RandomForestClassifier
from sklearn.metrics import accuracy_score
```

```
# Loading the data
data = load_wine()
X, y = data.data, data.target

# Splitting train/test sets
X_train, X_test, y_train, y_test = train_test_split(X, y,
test_size=0.2, random_state=42)

# Creating the classifier
model = RandomForestClassifier(n_estimators=100)

# Training the model
model.fit(X_train, y_train)

# Making predictions
y_pred = model.predict(X_test)

# Evaluation
accuracy = accuracy_score(y_test, y_pred)
print(f"Model Accuracy: {accuracy:.2f}")
```

Introduction to the Main

Classification Models in Scikit-Learn

Scikit-Learn provides several classification algorithms, each suitable for different types of data and scenarios. The most used models include:

Logistic Regression

Despite its name, logistic regression is a highly effective binary classification model. Its principle is based on the sigmoid function, which maps continuous values into probabilities belonging to two distinct classes.

python
```
from sklearn.linear_model import LogisticRegression

log_model = LogisticRegression()
log_model.fit(X_train, y_train)

predictions = log_model.predict(X_test)
```

Logistic regression is ideal for binary classification problems, such as spam detection and credit analysis.

Decision Trees

Decision trees segment data hierarchically, creating decision rules based on successive splits.

python
```
from sklearn.tree import DecisionTreeClassifier

tree_model = DecisionTreeClassifier(max_depth=3)
tree_model.fit(X_train, y_train)

predictions = tree_model.predict(X_test)
```

Decision trees are easy to interpret and useful for problems with clear decision rules.

Random Forest

Random Forest improves the stability and accuracy of decision trees by combining multiple trees into a more robust model.

python
```
from sklearn.ensemble import RandomForestClassifier
```

```
rf_model = RandomForestClassifier(n_estimators=100)
rf_model.fit(X_train, y_train)

predictions = rf_model.predict(X_test)
```

This model is widely used in applications requiring high performance and stability.

Support Vector Machines (SVM)

SVM aims to find a hyperplane that best separates classes, being highly effective in binary classification problems.

python
```
from sklearn.svm import SVC

svm_model = SVC(kernel='linear')
svm_model.fit(X_train, y_train)

predictions = svm_model.predict(X_test)
```

SVMs are efficient on complex datasets and with few samples.

K-Nearest Neighbors (KNN)

KNN classifies samples based on the proximity to the nearest neighbors.

python
```
from sklearn.neighbors import KNeighborsClassifier

knn_model = KNeighborsClassifier(n_neighbors=5)
knn_model.fit(X_train, y_train)

predictions = knn_model.predict(X_test)
```

KNN is ideal for problems where there is no clear relationship between predictors and the target variable.

Common Errors and Recommended Solutions

Error: "ValueError: Expected 2D array, got 1D array instead"
This error occurs when data is not properly structured.
Recommended Solution: Ensure that X and y are in the correct format. Use .reshape(-1, 1) when necessary.

Error: "NotFittedError: Estimator not fitted yet"
This error arises when trying to predict values without previously training the model.
Recommended Solution: Always execute .fit(X, y) before .predict(new_X).

Error: "ConvergenceWarning: lbfgs failed to converge"
This error occurs with logistic regression when the algorithm fails to find an optimal solution.
Recommended Solution: Increase the number of iterations with max_iter=500.

python
```
log_model = LogisticRegression(max_iter=500)
```

Best Practices and Real Applications

- Use Cross-Validation:
  The cross_val_score technique helps evaluate the model's stability across different subsets of data.
- Choose the Right Metric:

- For imbalanced datasets, use precision, recall, and f1-score instead of only accuracy.

- Normalize Data:

Models like SVM and logistic regression benefit from using StandardScaler() for data normalization.

python

```
from sklearn.preprocessing import StandardScaler

scaler = StandardScaler()
X_train_scaled = scaler.fit_transform(X_train)
X_test_scaled = scaler.transform(X_test)
```

Companies use classification models in various contexts, such as bank fraud detection, customer churn analysis, and personalized product recommendations.

Mastering classification models with Scikit-Learn allows you to transform large volumes of data into accurate predictions and strategic decisions. Each algorithm has distinct characteristics and advantages, and the correct choice depends on the type of data and the problem to be solved. Properly applying classification techniques ensures greater accuracy, reliability, and real impact on the results achieved.

CHAPTER 9. MODEL VALIDATION AND EVALUATION

Building Machine Learning models is not limited to training and generating predictions. To ensure that a model performs well and generalizes correctly to new data, it is essential to validate and evaluate it rigorously. Models that do not undergo proper validation tend to suffer from issues such as overfitting and underfitting, reducing their effectiveness when applied to real-world data.

Scikit-Learn offers a variety of techniques and metrics to evaluate models objectively and reliably. Mastering these concepts ensures the selection of more robust and effective models for different scenarios and applications.

Components, Templates, and Metadata

Scikit-Learn's validation and evaluation methods follow a modular and well-defined structure. They can be grouped into three main categories:

- **Cross-validation**: Tests the model on different subsets of data to check its stability and avoid issues like overfitting.

- **Evaluation metrics**: Determine the model's quality using statistical indicators specific to each type of problem.

- **Tuning and optimization techniques**: Improve model performance by adjusting hyperparameters and refining the data.

Each of these categories contains specific methods that follow a standardized flow within the library. This modular design allows for practical and efficient model evaluation and comparison.

Structural Directives and Attributes

To correctly evaluate a model in Scikit-Learn, some guidelines must be followed:

- Properly split the data into training and testing sets to avoid the model memorizing the training data.

- Use cross-validation to ensure that the results are consistent.

- Choose the correct evaluation metric, considering the type of problem (classification or regression).

- Avoid premature optimization without proper statistical validation.

Key internal attributes for model evaluation include:

- .score(): Returns the default evaluation metric for the model (accuracy for classification, R^2 for regression).

- .best_params_: Returns the best hyperparameters found in an optimized search.

- .cv_results_: Displays detailed results from cross-validation.

Practical usage example:

python
```
from sklearn.model_selection import train_test_split
```

```
from sklearn.ensemble import RandomForestClassifier
from sklearn.datasets import load_wine

# Loading data
data = load_wine()
X, y = data.data, data.target

# Splitting train/test
X_train, X_test, y_train, y_test = train_test_split(X, y,
test_size=0.2, random_state=42)

# Creating and training the model
model = RandomForestClassifier(n_estimators=100)
model.fit(X_train, y_train)

# Evaluating the model
accuracy = model.score(X_test, y_test)
print(f"Model accuracy: {accuracy:.2f}")
```

Introduction to Cross-Validation and Performance Evaluation Techniques

Cross-Validation

Cross-validation is an essential method to measure a model's generalization ability. Instead of splitting data into just one training and one test set, cross-validation splits the data into multiple parts and repeatedly tests the model on different subdivisions.

K-Fold Cross Validation

The most common method is K-Fold Cross Validation, which splits the data into K parts (or folds), training the model on K-1 parts and testing it on the remaining one. This process is repeated several times, ensuring a more robust evaluation.

python
```
from sklearn.model_selection import cross_val_score
from sklearn.ensemble import RandomForestClassifier
from sklearn.datasets import load_wine

# Loading data
data = load_wine()
X, y = data.data, data.target

# Creating the model
model = RandomForestClassifier(n_estimators=100)

# Executing cross-validation with 5 folds
results = cross_val_score(model, X, y, cv=5)

# Displaying average results
print(f"Average accuracy: {results.mean():.2f}")
```

This method reduces result variance and ensures the model isn't just benefiting from a particular data split.

Evaluation Metrics for Classification and Regression

The choice of the correct evaluation metric depends on the type of problem being solved.

Metrics for Classification

For classification problems, some essential metrics include:

- **Accuracy**: Measures the proportion of correct predictions relative to the total samples.

- **Precision and Recall**: Evaluate model performance on imbalanced data.

- **F1-Score**: Combines precision and recall into a single

balanced metric.

- **Confusion Matrix**: Analyzes classification errors in detail.

python
```python
from sklearn.metrics import classification_report
from sklearn.ensemble import RandomForestClassifier
from sklearn.datasets import load_wine
from sklearn.model_selection import train_test_split

# Loading and splitting data
data = load_wine()
X, y = data.data, data.target
X_train, X_test, y_train, y_test = train_test_split(X, y,
test_size=0.2, random_state=42)

# Training the model
model = RandomForestClassifier(n_estimators=100)
model.fit(X_train, y_train)

# Making predictions
y_pred = model.predict(X_test)

# Evaluation report
print(classification_report(y_test, y_pred))
```

Metrics for Regression

For regression problems, metrics such as absolute and squared errors are widely used:

- **R^2 (Coefficient of Determination)**: Measures the proportion of variability in the data explained by the model.

- **Mean Absolute Error (MAE)**: Measures the average error in absolute units.

- **Mean Squared Error (MSE)**: Penalizes larger errors more severely.

python
```
from sklearn.metrics import mean_absolute_error,
mean_squared_error, r2_score
from sklearn.linear_model import LinearRegression
from sklearn.datasets import load_diabetes
from sklearn.model_selection import train_test_split

# Loading data
data = load_diabetes()
X, y = data.data, data.target

# Splitting train/test
X_train, X_test, y_train, y_test = train_test_split(X, y,
test_size=0.2, random_state=42)

# Creating and training the model
model = LinearRegression()
model.fit(X_train, y_train)

# Making predictions
y_pred = model.predict(X_test)

# Evaluation
print(f"MAE: {mean_absolute_error(y_test, y_pred):.2f}")
print(f"MSE: {mean_squared_error(y_test, y_pred):.2f}")
print(f"R²: {r2_score(y_test, y_pred):.2f}")
```

Common Errors and Recommended Solutions

Error: "ValueError: X has 0 feature(s)"
Occurs when the model input lacks the correct dimensions.
Recommended Solution: Check the data format with .shape and use .reshape(-1, 1) if necessary.

Error: "UndefinedMetricWarning"
Happens when calculating metrics such as precision and recall on classes without samples.
Recommended Solution: Use the zero_division=1 option in classification_report to avoid this issue.

Error: "Overfitting during training"
When the model performs very well on training data but poorly on test data.
Recommended Solution: Use regularization or reduce model complexity.

Best Practices and Real Applications

- Always use cross-validation to ensure stable and reliable evaluations.

- Choose appropriate metrics for each type of problem, avoiding superficial analyses.

- Use regularization techniques to avoid overfitting models to training data.

Leading companies use validation and performance metrics to optimize demand forecasting models, fraud detection, and customer classification, ensuring reliability and high performance.

Mastering model validation and evaluation techniques ensures more reliable and impactful predictions. Properly using Scikit-Learn's metrics and methods provides greater precision and result stability, enabling more efficient and secure applications in real-world scenarios.

CHAPTER 10. HYPERPARAMETER TUNING

One of the most critical stages in developing efficient Machine Learning models is hyperparameter tuning. Hyperparameters are external values to the model, predefined, that directly influence the quality of the obtained predictions. Inadequate tuning can cause superficial and imprecise results or a high degree of overfitting, reducing the model's ability to generalize to new data.

Mastering hyperparameter tuning ensures that trained models are optimized for maximum efficiency and performance. Scikit-Learn offers specific and structured tools to simplify this critical process, allowing fine and automatic adjustments with precision and ease.

Components, Templates, and Metadata

In the context of hyperparameter tuning, Scikit-Learn uses highly effective modular components that are easily understood and applied due to their consistent internal structure. Each of these components is specifically designed to automatically optimize models.

Two main components used are:

- **GridSearchCV**: Performs a systematic search over all possible hyperparameter combinations.

- **RandomizedSearchCV**: Performs a random search, very efficient especially when the number of possible combinations is large.

These components are special estimators that take other estimators as input, testing different combinations of the provided parameters and automatically evaluating model quality through techniques like cross-validation.

Structural Directives and Attributes

Each component follows a standardized and easy-to-understand interface, ensuring rapid and consistent application in any technical context:

- **.fit(X, y)**: trains the estimator with different combinations of hyperparameters.

- **.best_params_**: returns the ideal combination of tested parameters.

- **.predict()**: automatically uses the model tuned with the best parameters found.

- **.cv_results_**: presents detailed results of each tested hyperparameter combination.

Practical example demonstrating the use of these structural directives:

```python
from sklearn.datasets import load_iris
from sklearn.svm import SVC
from sklearn.model_selection import GridSearchCV,
train_test_split

data = load_iris()
X, y = data.data, data.target
```

```
X_train, X_test, y_train, y_test = train_test_split(X, y,
test_size=0.2, random_state=42)

# Defining the parameter grid
parameters = {'C': [0.1, 1, 10],
              'gamma': [1, 0.1, 0.01],
              'kernel': ['linear', 'rbf']}

# Base estimator
svc_model = SVC()

# Optimized hyperparameter tuning
grid = GridSearchCV(svc_model, parameters, cv=5)
optimized_model = grid.fit(X_train, y_train)

# Displaying the best parameters found
print("Best parameters:", optimized_model.best_params_)
```

In this code, GridSearchCV automatically tests all provided parameter combinations, returning the best available configuration, ensuring precision and technical optimization.

Introduction to Optimized Hyperparameter Tuning

The hyperparameter tuning process essentially consists of finding the most suitable configurations for each estimator. This stage is crucial because model performance is directly influenced by the chosen values for these external parameters.

GridSearchCV: systematic search for the best parameters

GridSearchCV performs an exhaustive search over all specified parameters, using cross-validation to identify the configuration with the best performance.

Complete practical example using GridSearchCV:

python

```
from sklearn.ensemble import RandomForestClassifier
from sklearn.model_selection import GridSearchCV,
train_test_split
from sklearn.datasets import load_wine

data = load_wine()
X, y = data.data; data.target

# Splitting into train and test
X_train, X_test, y_train, y_test = train_test_split(X, y,
test_size=0.25)

# Defining parameters for testing
parameters = {'n_estimators': [10, 50, 100],
          'max_depth': [None, 10, 20],
          'min_samples_split': [2, 5, 10]}

# Instantiating base model
rf_model = RandomForestClassifier()

# GridSearch tuning
optimized_model = GridSearchCV(rf_model, parameters, cv=5)
optimized_model = optimized_model.fit(X_train, y_train)

# Detailed results
print("Optimized parameters:",
optimized_model.best_params_)
print("Best CV score:", optimized_model.best_score_)
```

This approach quickly finds the best possible set of parameters, ensuring technical effectiveness and maximum precision.

RandomizedSearchCV for large datasets

For large datasets, using a random search through RandomizedSearchCV can save considerable time while maintaining good performance.

python
```
from sklearn.model_selection import RandomizedSearchCV

# Random search of parameters
random_model = RandomizedSearchCV(rf_model, parameters, n_iter=10, cv=5)
optimized_model = random_model.fit(X_train, y_train)

print("Randomly chosen best-performing parameters:", optimized_model.best_params_)
```

Random search is particularly efficient when there are many possible parameters, allowing quick and effective results.

Common Errors and Recommended Solutions

Error: ValueError - Parameter does not exist in the model
Occurs when incorrect parameters are defined in GridSearchCV or RandomizedSearchCV.
Recommended Solution: Check the official Scikit-Learn documentation and confirm that all specified parameters are available for the chosen model.

Error: Excessive time or processing freeze
Happens when GridSearchCV tries to test too many combinations simultaneously.
Recommended Solution: Use RandomizedSearchCV or reduce the number of options and parameters tested simultaneously for faster results.

Error: "UndefinedMetricWarning"
Usually occurs when evaluating models with highly imbalanced data.
Recommended Solution: Use alternative metrics like F1-Score, Recall, or ROC-AUC, which are more appropriate for imbalanced data.

Best Practices and Real Applications

- Always use complete pipelines integrating preprocessing and parameter tuning, ensuring automation and reproducibility.

- Choose evaluation metrics compatible with the model's final goal, especially in specific problems like imbalanced data.

- Consider the cost-benefit between computational time and performance improvement when selecting tuning methods.

Large organizations, such as financial institutions and leading technology companies, rigorously apply hyperparameter tuning to continuously optimize their models, especially in areas like risk analysis, personalized recommendation, and digital security.

Mastering optimized hyperparameter tuning techniques is fundamental to ensure robust, efficient models capable of correctly generalizing to practical situations. Using the detailed tools ensures technical precision, productivity, and consistent results, positioning you to face any Machine Learning challenge with confidence and technical clarity.

CHAPTER 11. ENSEMBLE METHODS

Ensemble methods are advanced approaches in Machine Learning that combine multiple simple models, known as base models, to create a final model that is more robust, stable, and highly accurate. The logic behind this approach is that different models have different strengths and weaknesses; by combining them, it is possible to reduce the risk of individual errors and significantly increase overall predictive capability.

Scikit-Learn offers several clear and standardized implementations of Ensemble techniques, making it accessible to use these models in different contexts. Two very popular and frequently used techniques are Random Forest and Gradient Boosting. Each of these techniques offers unique characteristics, making them suitable for specific problems, complex scenarios, or large volumes of data.

Components, Templates, and Metadata

Ensemble methods are composed of multiple strategically combined estimators, generating predictions based on the aggregation of individual model results. Each estimator used in ensemble methods follows the same standardized Scikit-Learn interface, mandatorily having the .fit() and .predict() methods.

In Scikit-Learn, ensemble methods are divided into two main categories:

- Bagging Methods (such as Random Forest);

- Boosting Methods (such as Gradient Boosting and AdaBoost).

Bagging (Bootstrap Aggregating)

Bagging generates multiple models trained with different subsets of the original data, obtained through sampling with replacement. The final result is obtained by aggregating (usually majority voting or averaging) the predictions of the individual models.

Boosting (Adaptive Boosting)

Boosting builds a sequential series of models, where each new model seeks to correct the errors of the previous one. The goal is to continuously improve performance by correcting specific errors identified in earlier steps.

Random Forest

Random Forest is an advanced version of Bagging, applying multiple decision trees trained on random subsets of the data and explanatory variables. This approach produces high stability and robustness for complex problems.

Detailed code demonstrating RandomForestClassifier:

python

```
from sklearn.ensemble import RandomForestClassifier
from sklearn.datasets import load_breast_cancer
from sklearn.model_selection import train_test_split
from sklearn.metrics import accuracy_score

data = load_breast_cancer()
X, y = data.data, data.target

X_train, X_test, y_train, y_test = train_test_split(X, y,
test_size=0.2, random_state=42)
```

```
rf_model = RandomForestClassifier(n_estimators=100,
random_state=42)
rf_model.fit(X_train, y_train)

y_pred = rf_model.predict(X_test)
accuracy = accuracy_score(y_test, y_pred)
print("RandomForest Accuracy:", accuracy)
```

The code above generates accurate predictions in complex binary problems with a fast and effective approach.

Structural Directives and Attributes

Ensemble methods share specific structural directives that must be clearly understood for correct and optimized application:

- Every ensemble model must be instantiated before training, choosing essential parameters like the number of estimators (n_estimators) correctly.

- The .fit() step always precedes .predict().

- Relevant internal attributes, such as .feature_importances_ in RandomForest, allow understanding which variables are most important in the final model.

Introduction to Ensemble Methods: Random Forest and Gradient Boosting

Random Forest

Random Forest is particularly effective at reducing variance, avoiding overfitting compared to isolated trees. Composed of several independent decision trees, each tree uses a random set of variables and data for training.

Gradient Boosting

Gradient Boosting, unlike Random Forest, builds models sequentially, each focused on correcting the errors made by the previous model. This approach ensures high accuracy, especially in large datasets.

Practical code for GradientBoostingClassifier:

python

```
from sklearn.ensemble import GradientBoostingClassifier

gb_model = GradientBoostingClassifier(n_estimators=100,
learning_rate=0.1, random_state=42)
gb_model.fit(X_train, y_train)

y_pred = gb_model.predict(X_test)
accuracy = accuracy_score(y_test, y_pred)
print("Gradient Boosting Accuracy:", accuracy)
```

Both methods offer accurate results, but Gradient Boosting requires greater attention to avoid overfitting.

Common Errors and Recommended Solutions

Error: High Variance (Overfitting) in Random Forest
Random Forest may overly adapt to the training set, reducing overall performance on test data.
Recommended Solution:

- Reduce maximum depth (max_depth) or increase the minimum number of samples per leaf (min_samples_leaf).

- Use cross-validation frequently.

Error: Excessive training time
Methods like Random Forest or Gradient Boosting can take a long time with extensive datasets.

Recommended Solutions:

- Initially reduce the number of estimators, analyzing the cost-benefit.

- Use optimized algorithms such as HistGradientBoostingClassifier, which has faster performance.

Error: Evident Overfitting in Gradient Boosting
Gradient Boosting may overfit the training data, losing generalization ability.

Recommended Solutions:

- Use rigorous cross-validation.

- Adjust hyperparameters like max_depth, learning_rate, and reduce the number of estimators (n_estimators) to avoid excessive complexity.

Best Practices and Real Applications

- When using ensemble, frequently check feature importance with .feature_importances_ to better understand the models.

- Combine different ensemble models (e.g., Random Forest and Gradient Boosting) to capture multiple types of relationships in the data.

- Always validate results with cross-validation techniques

to prevent complex models from overfitting.

Real applications of these methods include:

- Financial institutions use Random Forest for risk analysis and fraud detection, ensuring technical accuracy and security.

- Technology companies apply Gradient Boosting for advanced recommendation systems and content personalization, enabling fast and effective predictions.

- Healthcare sectors adopt ensemble models for early and precise diagnoses based on large volumes of medical data.

Mastering Ensemble methods provides significant advantages in complex Machine Learning scenarios. By using modular Scikit-Learn components like Random Forest or Gradient Boosting, you directly increase the robustness, stability, and technical accuracy of your models. The detailed understanding presented in this chapter on construction, usage, optimization, and practical application of these methods guarantees maximum operational efficiency and technical effectiveness in any Machine Learning project you undertake.

CHAPTER 12. SUPPORT VECTOR MACHINES (SVM)

Support Vector Machines (SVM) are essential algorithms in the context of Machine Learning, especially recognized for their effectiveness in classification problems, although they can also be applied to regression tasks. They stand out for their ability to identify optimal hyperplanes for clear separation between distinct classes, presenting significant robustness even with complex and difficult-to-classify datasets.

SVM offers clear technical advantages such as robustness to noise, excellent generalization ability, and efficiency in high dimensionality, making them widely applied in critical areas such as recommendation systems, medical image classification, financial fraud detection, and text recognition.

In this context, deeply understanding the structural components, practical application, and the main attributes and methods of the SVM model in Scikit-Learn becomes a fundamental competence for data scientists and analysts.

Components, Templates, and Metadata

In Scikit-Learn, Support Vector Machines are implemented through the standard SVC class for classification problems, or SVR for regression problems. These models follow the consistent and modular structure characteristic of the library, facilitating their use and integration with other Machine Learning tools and techniques.

The practical use of the SVM model implies a clear understanding of the fundamental methods of the interface:

- **.fit(X, y)**: essential method that performs learning from the provided data.

- **.predict(new_X)**: used after learning to make predictions on new datasets.

- **.score(X_test, y_test)**: provides a quick and direct metric about the quality of the trained model.

This method structure is common to all models in Scikit-Learn, allowing easy integration with automated pipelines and technical consistency in Machine Learning operations.

Structural Directives and Attributes

In Scikit-Learn, SVMs follow structural directives that ensure standardization and clarity in their implementation and use. It is necessary to clearly understand each attribute and structural directive of SVM classifiers to successfully apply these models.

Main structural attributes of a trained SVM model:

- **support_vectors_**: array with the most important points that define the decision boundary, called support vectors.

- **coef_**: weights associated with each feature of the input variables (valid for linear kernels).

- **intercept_**: point where the hyperplane cuts the axis, helping define the model's exact decisions.

Standard implementation using the SVC class with a linear kernel:

python

```python
from sklearn.datasets import load_iris
from sklearn.model_selection import train_test_split
from sklearn.svm import SVC
from sklearn.metrics import accuracy_score

data = load_iris()
X, y = data.data, data.target

# Splitting the data into train and test sets
X_train, X_test, y_train, y_test = train_test_split(X, y,
test_size=0.3)

# SVM model with linear kernel
svm_model = SVC(kernel='linear', C=1.0)

# Training the model
svm_model.fit(X_train, y_train)

# Making predictions with new data
y_pred = svm_model.predict(X_test)

# Performance evaluation
accuracy = accuracy_score(y_test, y_pred)
print(f"SVM Accuracy: {accuracy:.2f}")
```

In the code above, the linear kernel was selected for simplicity and clear initial performance. Other types of kernels (rbf, poly, sigmoid) are also offered by Scikit-Learn, allowing the model to be adjusted to complex data with different types of relationships.

Introduction to the Use of Support Vector Machines

Support Vector Machines operate by precisely defining an ideal hyperplane for class separation. The hyperplane is positioned to maximize the distance (margin) between the different classes in the data.

Hyperplane and Decision Margins

When defining hyperplanes, SVMs establish clear margins that separate classes with maximum clarity. The quality of separation directly depends on the correct configuration of the kernel and main parameters such as C and gamma.

Types of Kernels and Their Applications

Scikit-Learn provides different types of kernels that define the behavior and flexibility of SVMs. The main ones are:

- **Linear**: simplest and ideal for linearly separable data.

- **Polynomial (poly)**: effective when data have polynomial relationships.

- **RBF (Radial Basis Function)**: ideal for complex and nonlinear data, widely used in practice.

- **Sigmoid**: mainly used in neural networks and rarely applied in conventional classification problems.

Example with RBF kernel, highly used in complex and nonlinear situations:

python
```
svm_rbf = SVC(kernel='rbf', C=1.0, gamma='scale')

svm_rbf.fit(X_train, y_train)
predictions = svm_rbf.predict(X_test)
print("Accuracy with RBF kernel:", accuracy_score(y_test, predictions))
```

Common Errors and Recommended Solutions

Error: Model extremely slow or with no apparent convergence
When an SVM model takes excessively long, it usually indicates issues with the gamma hyperparameter value or data scaling.
Recommended Solution: Use StandardScaler to normalize data before training:

python
```
from sklearn.preprocessing import StandardScaler

scaler = StandardScaler()
X_train_scaled = scaler.fit_transform(X_train)
X_test_scaled = scaler.transform(X_test)

svm_model.fit(X_train_scaled, y_train)
```

Error: Completely incorrect predictions with polynomial or RBF kernel
This error often arises when the kernel is poorly defined for the data type in use.
Recommended Solution: Test first with a linear kernel to check initial performance. If necessary, use GridSearchCV to automatically find ideal hyperparameters.

Error: "ValueError: C must be positive"
This error occurs when the hyperparameter C is incorrectly set to negative values or zero.
Recommended Solution: Always define C as a positive value greater than zero, adjusting with cross-validation if necessary.

Best Practices and Real Applications

- Always use cross-validation for robust SVM evaluation, ensuring the model is not suffering from overfitting or underfitting.

- Initially evaluate with a linear kernel; if there is no good separation, explore the RBF kernel, especially with complex data.

- Consider optimizing hyperparameters using GridSearchCV or RandomizedSearchCV, facilitating detailed and precise SVM model tuning.

Practical applications of SVMs include:

- Spam detection in email systems.

- Classification and recognition of medical images, such as X-rays.

- Text analysis and voice recognition on technology platforms.

Deeply understanding Support Vector Machines (SVM) enables the creation of efficient, robust, and accurate models for complex classification tasks. By properly applying structural directives, hyperparameters, and validations, you ensure high-performance models capable of generating impactful, real-world results of great value in technical, scientific, and commercial contexts.

CHAPTER 13. NEURAL NETWORKS WITH SCIKIT-LEARN (MLPCLASSIFIER)

Neural networks are powerful and widely used tools in Machine Learning due to their ability to identify complex patterns in large volumes of data. Scikit-Learn offers a clear and intuitive implementation of simple neural networks through the MLPClassifier (Multi-Layer Perceptron Classifier) component. This implementation allows you to create and train neural models with effectiveness, speed, and technical efficiency.

The MLPClassifier is an advanced model that can be used in various applications such as image classification, financial forecasting, fraud detection, and predictive analytics. Understanding the construction and practical use of these networks ensures greater efficiency and consistent results in any professional context.

Components, Templates, and Metadata

Scikit-Learn provides well-defined and modular components to create and train neural networks using MLPClassifier. This classifier implements neural networks with multiple hidden layers, capable of capturing complex nonlinear relationships between variables.

Main components and fundamental methods used in MLPClassifier are:

- **fit(X, y)**: trains the model with the provided data, adjusting the internal weights of the neural layers.

- **predict(X)**: makes predictions on new datasets after training.

- **score(X, y)**: quickly evaluates the model's performance on provided data, returning overall accuracy.

- **predict_proba(X)**: provides the probability estimates for each class predicted by the model.

This modular structure allows easy integration with other steps of Machine Learning processes, such as cross-validation, feature selection, and automated pipelines, ensuring technical efficiency throughout the workflow.

Structural Directives and Attributes

MLPClassifier uses specific internal attributes, which are essential for understanding the structure of the trained model and optimizing its operations:

- **coefs_**: trained weights for each layer of the model after training.

- **intercepts_**: intercept values for each neuron, fundamental for precisely defining the activation functions.

- **n_iter_**: total number of iterations performed during training.

- **loss_curve_**: loss curve, used to evaluate and monitor performance and convergence during training.

A detailed practical implementation:

python

```python
from sklearn.datasets import load_iris
from sklearn.neural_network import MLPClassifier
from sklearn.model_selection import train_test_split
from sklearn.metrics import accuracy_score

# Loading dataset
data = load_iris()
X, y = data.data, data.target

# Splitting the data
X_train, X_test, y_train, y_test = train_test_split(X, y,
test_size=0.2, random_state=42)

# Instantiating the MLPClassifier
mlp      =      MLPClassifier(hidden_layer_sizes=(10,      10),
max_iter=1000, random_state=42)

# Training
mlp.fit(X_train, y_train)

# Prediction
predictions = mlp.predict(X_test)

# Accuracy evaluation
print("Neural   Network   Accuracy:",   accuracy_score(y_test,
predictions))
```

Here, a simple neural network was created with two hidden layers of 10 neurons each. Training occurs up to a maximum of 1000 iterations, ensuring the model has enough time to properly learn.

Introduction to Creating and

Training Simple Neural Networks

Creating simple neural networks starts with clearly defining the internal architecture, number of layers, and number of neurons. In general, it is advisable to start with simple structures and gradually increase complexity, carefully evaluating performance.

Detailed example creating a simple neural network:

python

```
mlp_simple = MLPClassifier(hidden_layer_sizes=(5,),
activation='relu', solver='adam', max_iter=500)
mlp_simple.fit(X_train, y_train)
simple_predictions = mlp_simple.predict(X_test)
simple_accuracy = accuracy_score(y_test, simple_predictions)

print("Simple network accuracy:", simple_accuracy)
```

Common Activation Functions

MLPClassifier allows you to define different activation functions that determine the behavior of neurons in the hidden layers. The most commonly used functions are:

- **relu (Rectified Linear Unit)**: fast convergence and widely recommended as an initial default.

- **tanh (Hyperbolic Tangent)**: outputs between -1 and 1, suitable for smaller networks.

- **logistic**: sigmoid function that limits values between 0 and 1, traditional in binary classification problems.

Changing the activation function can directly impact the neural network's performance, allowing specific adjustments according to the context.

Common Errors and Recommended Solutions

Error: ConvergenceWarning – Maximum iteration reached without convergence
Occurs frequently when the maximum number of iterations is insufficient for complete training.
Recommended Solutions:

- Increase max_iter to values higher than 1000.

- Use data normalization to speed up convergence with StandardScaler.

python
```
from sklearn.preprocessing import StandardScaler

scaler = StandardScaler()
X_train_norm = scaler.fit_transform(X_train)
X_test_norm = scaler.transform(X_test)

mlp = MLPClassifier(max_iter=1500)
mlp.fit(X_train_norm, y_train)
```

Error: Poor accuracy due to feature scale
Neural networks are sensitive to data scaling, especially with ReLU activation.
Recommended Solution: Normalize or standardize the data using StandardScaler or MinMaxScaler to ensure all variables are on similar scales.

python
```
from sklearn.preprocessing import MinMaxScaler

scaler = MinMaxScaler()
X_train = scaler.fit_transform(X_train)
```

```
X_test = scaler.transform(X_test)
```

Error: Evident Overfitting (High training accuracy and low testing accuracy)
Overfitting can occur with neural networks when they are too complex or trained for too long.
Recommended Solutions:

- Reduce the number of neurons or hidden layers to simplify the network.

- Use regularization techniques, such as alpha in MLPClassifier:

python
```
mlp_regularized = MLPClassifier(hidden_layer_sizes=(10,),
alpha=0.01)
```

Best Practices and Real Applications

- Always normalize data before training neural networks.

- Regularly monitor the loss curve (**loss_curve_**) to detect problems during training.

- Frequently use cross-validation to verify network stability and generalization.

- Use early stopping techniques to automatically end training when no further performance gains are observed.

Real-world practical applications:

- Banks and financial institutions apply simple neural

networks for credit risk prediction.

- Hospitals use MLPClassifier to assist in quick and reliable diagnostics based on clinical exams.

- Technology platforms use neural networks for personalized content and product recommendations.

Use and training of simple neural networks with Scikit-Learn (MLPClassifier) offers immediate practical possibilities, providing powerful and accurate models. By properly applying the detailed concepts, you will be able to generate practical, effective, and technically robust solutions across a wide range of critical applications, creating a significant technical advantage in your Machine Learning solutions.

Chapter 14. Clustering Algorithms

Clustering is an unsupervised Machine Learning technique that identifies hidden patterns in data by grouping similar instances based on their characteristics. Unlike classification, where class labels are known, clustering algorithms analyze data without prior supervision, autonomously discovering patterns. This approach is widely used in customer segmentation, anomaly detection, document clustering, and bioinformatics.

Scikit-Learn offers several efficient implementations of clustering algorithms, enabling data scientists and engineers to apply these techniques quickly and scalably.

Components, Templates, and Metadata

Clustering algorithms in Scikit-Learn follow a consistent modular structure. Each algorithm implements fundamental methods for fitting and prediction:

- **fit(X)**: analyzes the data and finds clustering patterns.

- **predict(new_X)**: assigns new points to already identified clusters (not all models support this functionality).

- **fit_predict(X)**: fits the model and directly returns the labels assigned to each sample.

Additionally, each algorithm has specific attributes:

- **labels_**: labels assigned to each point after training.

- **cluster_centers_**: coordinates of the cluster centers, when applicable.

- **inertia_**: a measure of cluster cohesion, useful for

optimization.

Clustering is used for many practical applications, such as customer segmentation in retail and pattern discovery in large-scale datasets.

Structural Directives and Attributes

The main clustering algorithms available in Scikit-Learn are:

- **K-Means**: popular and efficient, partitions data into a predefined number of groups.

- **DBSCAN**: detects clusters of different densities and handles outliers well.

- **Agglomerative Clustering**: hierarchical approach to finding natural groupings in data.

- **Mean Shift**: detects clusters based on data density, without needing to define a fixed number of groups.

Each of these algorithms has specific characteristics that must be considered when choosing the best approach for a specific problem.

Example of clustering using K-Means:

python
```
from sklearn.cluster import KMeans
from sklearn.datasets import make_blobs

# Generating synthetic data
X, _ = make_blobs(n_samples=300, centers=4, cluster_std=0.6,
random_state=42)

# Creating and training the K-Means model
```

```
kmeans_model = KMeans(n_clusters=4, random_state=42)
kmeans_model.fit(X)

# Viewing the cluster labels
print("Assigned labels:", kmeans_model.labels_)
print("Cluster centers:", kmeans_model.cluster_centers_)
```

In this example, K-Means partitions the data into 4 clusters, assigning a label to each sample based on proximity to the calculated centers.

Introduction to Clustering and Its Main Algorithms

K-Means

K-Means is one of the most widely used algorithms due to its simplicity and efficiency. It works iteratively, assigning each point to the nearest centroid and recalculating centers until stability is reached.

Detailed code:

python
```
from sklearn.cluster import KMeans
from sklearn.datasets import make_blobs

# Creating synthetic data
X, _ = make_blobs(n_samples=500, centers=3, cluster_std=1.0,
random_state=42)

# Applying K-Means with 3 clusters
model = KMeans(n_clusters=3, random_state=42)
model.fit(X)

# Assigning labels to data
```

```
labels = model.predict(X)
print("Cluster labels:", labels)
```

K-Means is widely used in customer segmentation, document organization, and pattern recognition.

DBSCAN

DBSCAN (Density-Based Spatial Clustering of Applications with Noise) is a density-based algorithm that detects clusters with different shapes and can identify outliers.

python
```
from sklearn.cluster import DBSCAN

# Creating and training the DBSCAN model
dbscan_model = DBSCAN(eps=0.5, min_samples=5)
dbscan_model.fit(X)

# Viewing assigned labels
print("Cluster labels:", dbscan_model.labels_)
```

DBSCAN is useful in scenarios where data has variable cluster sizes and there is no need to specify the exact number of groups.

Agglomerative Clustering

This hierarchical method progressively groups points, merging the closest ones into larger clusters until a complete structure is formed.

python
```
from sklearn.cluster import AgglomerativeClustering

# Creating the hierarchical clustering model
```

```python
agglomerative_model = AgglomerativeClustering(n_clusters=3)
agglomerative_model.fit(X)

# Obtaining labels
print("Cluster labels:", agglomerative_model.labels_)
```

Hierarchical clustering is often used in bioinformatics and social network analysis.

Common Errors and Recommended Solutions

Error: "ValueError: Number of clusters should be > 0"
Occurs when an invalid value is passed to n_clusters.
Recommended Solution: Make sure to define n_clusters with a positive and appropriate number for the data.

Error: K-Means does not converge
If the K-Means model does not reach convergence, clusters may not be representative.
Recommended Solution: Increase max_iter to allow more adjustment iterations.

python
```python
model = KMeans(n_clusters=3, max_iter=500)
```

Error: DBSCAN classifies all points as noise (-1)
If many points are labeled as -1, it means eps or min_samples are not well adjusted.
Recommended Solution: Reduce eps or decrease min_samples to improve cluster detection.

python
```python
dbscan_model = DBSCAN(eps=0.3, min_samples=3)
```

Best Practices and Real Applications

- Use evaluation metrics such as the Silhouette Coefficient (silhouette_score) to measure clustering quality.

- Choose the correct algorithm based on the data's distribution and characteristics.

- Normalize data before clustering to prevent variables with different scales from affecting the results.

Practical applications include:

- Customer segmentation for personalized marketing campaigns.

- Anomaly detection in financial systems for fraud identification.

- Document clustering for optimizing searches in large databases.

Clustering is a powerful tool for finding hidden patterns in data and can be applied across many fields of knowledge. Each algorithm has its advantages and challenges, and the correct choice depends on the type of data and the problem to be solved. Mastery of these techniques enables the creation of intelligent and efficient solutions, becoming a strategic differentiator in modeling complex data.

CHAPTER 15. DIMENSIONALITY REDUCTION

Dimensionality reduction is a fundamental technique in Machine Learning and data analysis, allowing for the optimization of information representation by removing redundant or irrelevant variables. This approach improves computational efficiency, reduces the risk of overfitting, and facilitates data interpretation, especially in datasets with many variables.

Scikit-Learn offers robust methods for dimensionality reduction, including Principal Component Analysis (PCA) and t-Distributed Stochastic Neighbor Embedding (t-SNE). The first is widely used for data compression and improvement of predictive models, while the second is ideal for exploratory visualizations and detection of complex patterns.

Components, Templates, and Metadata

Dimensionality reduction methods in Scikit-Learn follow a well-defined flow. Each technique has specific components that determine how the data will be transformed and represented.

The main methods include:

- **PCA (Principal Component Analysis)**: transforms the data into a new space where variables are projected to maximize variance, preserving as much information as possible.

- **t-SNE (t-Distributed Stochastic Neighbor Embedding)**:

reduces dimensionality focusing on preserving the local structure of the data, highly effective for 2D or 3D visualizations.

Each method follows the modular structure of Scikit-Learn and provides fundamental methods:

- **.fit(X)**: fits the model to the data structure.

- **.transform(X)**: applies the transformation and reduces dimensionality.

- **.fit_transform(X)**: performs both processes simultaneously.

These methods guarantee flexible and efficient application for model optimization and exploration of high-dimensional data.

Structural Directives and Attributes

Each dimensionality reduction technique has specific structural directives, ensuring that the data is properly handled before transformation.

Main model attributes:

PCA

- **explained_variance_ratio_**: indicates the amount of variance explained by each principal component.

- **components_**: matrix that defines the new axes of the transformed space.

- **n_components_**: number of components used for projection.

t-SNE

- **n_components**: defines the new dimensionality of the reduced data.

- **perplexity**: controls how relationships between points are preserved.

- **learning_rate**: adjusts the model's convergence.

Practical code applying PCA:

python
```python
from sklearn.decomposition import PCA
from sklearn.datasets import load_digits
import matplotlib.pyplot as plt

# Loading the data
data = load_digits()
X = data.data

# Applying PCA to reduce to 2 principal components
pca = PCA(n_components=2)
X_reduced = pca.fit_transform(X)

# Visualizing the components
plt.scatter(X_reduced[:, 0], X_reduced[:, 1], c=data.target,
cmap='viridis')
plt.colorbar()
plt.title("Data Visualization with PCA")
plt.show()
```

In this code, the data is reduced to two dimensions, facilitating exploratory visualization and analysis.

Introduction to Dimensionality

Reduction with PCA and t-SNE

Dimensionality reduction is essential when a dataset has too many variables, making analysis and efficient modeling difficult. Two widely used methods in Scikit-Learn are PCA and t-SNE.

PCA (Principal Component Analysis)

PCA reduces dimensionality by projecting the data into a new space where information variance is maximized. It is useful for improving predictive model efficiency and eliminating redundancies.

Code for dimensionality reduction with PCA:

python
```
from sklearn.decomposition import PCA
from sklearn.datasets import load_iris

# Loading the data
data = load_iris()
X = data.data

# Applying PCA
pca = PCA(n_components=2)
X_pca = pca.fit_transform(X)

print("Explained variance:", pca.explained_variance_ratio_)
```

This method retains most of the information present in the original data, ensuring efficiency and simplification in modeling.

t-SNE (t-Distributed Stochastic Neighbor Embedding)

t-SNE is a nonlinear technique that reduces dimensionality by emphasizing the preservation of local relationships between points, making it useful for detailed visualizations.

Practical code using t-SNE:

python
```
from sklearn.manifold import TSNE

# Applying t-SNE
tsne = TSNE(n_components=2, perplexity=30,
learning_rate=200, random_state=42)
X_tsne = tsne.fit_transform(X)

# Visualizing the clusters
plt.scatter(X_tsne[:, 0], X_tsne[:, 1], c=data.target,
cmap='viridis')
plt.colorbar()
plt.title("Visualization with t-SNE")
plt.show()
```

t-SNE is highly recommended for exploring and visualizing high-dimensional data, especially in classification problems.

Common Errors and Recommended Solutions

Error: "ValueError: n_components must be between 0 and min(n_samples, n_features)"
This error occurs when the number of components chosen for PCA is greater than the number of available dimensions.
Recommended Solution: Define an appropriate number of components, respecting the dimensionality of the data:

python
```
pca = PCA(n_components=3)
```

Error: t-SNE very slow on large datasets

t-SNE can be extremely slow when applied to datasets with many records.

Recommended Solution: Use PCA before t-SNE to reduce the initial dimensionality and accelerate execution.

python

```
X_pca = PCA(n_components=50).fit_transform(X)
X_tsne = TSNE(n_components=2).fit_transform(X_pca)
```

Error: Incorrect interpretation of explained variance in PCA
A common mistake is to assume that only a fixed number of components is always the best choice.

Recommended Solution: Evaluate the explained variance before defining n_components:

python

```
pca = PCA().fit(X)
print("Cumulative explained variance:",
pca.explained_variance_ratio_.cumsum())
```

This approach allows determining the ideal number of components to ensure maximum information retention.

Best Practices and Real Applications

- Always normalize the data before applying PCA to prevent variables on different scales from affecting the reduction.

- Use PCA to remove redundancies before training predictive models, optimizing learning efficiency.

- Use t-SNE only for visualizations and not for preprocessing before Machine Learning models.

Real applications of these techniques include:

- Image analysis and pattern recognition, reducing the dimensionality of images to facilitate classification.

- Customer segmentation, grouping consumers based on characteristics reduced to principal components.

- Variable reduction in IoT sensors, enabling quick and efficient analysis of large-volume time series.

Dimensionality reduction plays an essential role in optimizing Machine Learning models and visualizing complex data. PCA and t-SNE are powerful tools that ensure greater efficiency, better data interpretation, and modeling optimization. By correctly applying these techniques, it is possible to transform large volumes of data into simpler and more effective representations, significantly improving analysis quality and predictive results.

CHAPTER 16. ANOMALY DETECTION

Anomaly detection is an essential technique in Machine Learning for identifying patterns that deviate from the normal behavior of a dataset. These anomalies can indicate financial fraud, system failures, cyberattacks, or any other unusual event that requires attention. Unlike traditional classification, where class labels are clearly defined, anomaly detection often operates with unlabeled data, using unsupervised approaches to detect unexpected patterns.

Scikit-Learn offers robust tools for anomaly detection, including Isolation Forest, Local Outlier Factor (LOF), and One-Class SVM. Each method has specific advantages depending on the analysis context.

Components, Templates, and Metadata

Anomaly detection algorithms in Scikit-Learn follow the library's traditional modular structure. Each model implements fundamental methods that allow fitting, predicting, and interpreting the results of anomaly analysis.

The main methods include:

- **Isolation Forest**: a decision tree-based algorithm that isolates anomalies faster than conventional methods.

- **Local Outlier Factor (LOF)**: measures the density of points and detects those isolated relative to the rest of the dataset.

- **One-Class SVM**: a model based on Support Vector Machines (SVM) that learns a decision boundary to distinguish normal patterns from anomalies.

These algorithms follow the standard Scikit-Learn interface:

- **.fit(X)**: fits the model to the provided data.

- **.predict(X)**: classifies points as normal or anomalous (-1 indicates anomaly).

- **.decision_function(X)**: returns the anomaly score for each point.

Basic example of anomaly detection with Isolation Forest:

python
```
from sklearn.ensemble import IsolationForest
import numpy as np

# Creating simulated data
X = np.random.randn(100, 2)

# Inserting manual anomalies
X[95:] = X[95:] + 5

# Creating and training the Isolation Forest model
model = IsolationForest(contamination=0.05,
random_state=42)
model.fit(X)

# Predicting anomalies
y_pred = model.predict(X)

# Displaying the number of anomalies detected
```

```
print("Total anomalies detected:", sum(y_pred == -1))
```

In this code, Isolation Forest identifies anomalies in a simulated dataset, detecting points that deviate from the expected distribution.

Structural Directives and Attributes

Each anomaly detection method has important attributes that assist in interpreting and optimizing the models.

Main model attributes:

Isolation Forest

- **estimators_**: individual decision trees used in detection.

- **threshold_**: threshold value used to determine if a point is an anomaly.

Local Outlier Factor (LOF)

- **negative_outlier_factor_**: indicates the degree of anomaly for each point, with smaller negative values associated with a higher probability of being anomalous.

One-Class SVM

- **support_vectors_**: support vectors used to define the decision boundary.

Code for anomaly analysis with LOF:

python

```
from sklearn.neighbors import LocalOutlierFactor
```

```
# Creating LOF model
lof_model = LocalOutlierFactor(n_neighbors=20,
contamination=0.05)

# Fitting and predicting anomalies
y_lof = lof_model.fit_predict(X)

# Counting anomalies detected
print("Total anomalies detected by LOF:", sum(y_lof == -1))
```

The **negative_outlier_factor_** metric can be used to interpret the intensity of detected anomalies.

Introduction to Anomaly Detection with Isolation Forest and Other Methods

Anomaly detection is fundamental in many sectors, as it allows for the identification of suspicious patterns or failures before they cause significant impacts. In Scikit-Learn, different algorithms meet specific needs:

Isolation Forest isolates data points randomly in decision trees and measures how many splits are required to isolate them. Points that require fewer splits are more likely to be anomalies.

Detailed code using Isolation Forest:

python

```
from sklearn.ensemble import IsolationForest
import numpy as np

# Generating normal data
X = np.random.normal(0, 1, (100, 2))

# Adding anomalies
```

```python
X_anomaly = np.random.normal(5, 1, (5, 2))
X = np.vstack([X, X_anomaly])

# Training the model
model = IsolationForest(contamination=0.05)
model.fit(X)

# Identifying anomalies
y_pred = model.predict(X)
print("Anomalies detected:", sum(y_pred == -1))
```

LOF compares the density of a point relative to its neighbors. Very different values indicate possible anomalies.

Code for LOF:

python

```python
from sklearn.neighbors import LocalOutlierFactor

lof_model = LocalOutlierFactor(n_neighbors=20,
contamination=0.05)
y_lof = lof_model.fit_predict(X)

print("Anomalies detected by LOF:", sum(y_lof == -1))
```

One-Class SVM models a decision surface to separate normal instances from anomalies. It works well in situations where there are few examples of anomalies available.

python

```python
from sklearn.svm import OneClassSVM

svm_model = OneClassSVM(nu=0.05, kernel="rbf")
svm_model.fit(X)
```

```
y_svm = svm_model.predict(X)
print("Anomalies detected by One-Class SVM:", sum(y_svm ==
-1))
```

Common Errors and Recommended Solutions

Error: "ValueError: Contamination must be between 0 and 0.5"
Occurs when the contamination rate is defined outside the recommended range.
Recommended Solution: Set a value between 0 and 0.5, representing the expected proportion of anomalies in the dataset.

python
```
model = IsolationForest(contamination=0.1)
```

Error: Anomalies not correctly detected
If a method does not properly identify anomalies, hyperparameters may need adjustment.
Recommended Solution: Adjust n_neighbors in LOF, contamination in Isolation Forest, or nu in One-Class SVM to improve sensitivity.

python
```
lof_model = LocalOutlierFactor(n_neighbors=10,
contamination=0.02)
```

Error: Excessive training time
Algorithms like LOF and One-Class SVM can be slow for large datasets.
Recommended Solution: Use random sampling to reduce the dataset size before training.

python
```
X_sample = X[np.random.choice(X.shape[0], 500,
replace=False)]
```

Best Practices and Real Applications

- Combine different methods to validate anomaly detection.

- Adjust hyperparameters according to data distribution to avoid false positives.

- Use scatter plots to visualize anomalies in two-dimensional problems.

- Evaluate the false positive rate before deploying an anomaly detection model in production.

Real applications include:

- Financial fraud detection for suspicious transactions on credit cards.

- Network monitoring and cybersecurity, identifying abnormal accesses and activities.

- Predictive maintenance in factories, preventing equipment failures through sensor analysis.

Anomaly detection plays a fundamental role in various fields, preventing risks and optimizing processes. Scikit-Learn provides efficient tools like Isolation Forest, LOF, and One-Class SVM, allowing for detailed and reliable analyses. By correctly applying these techniques, it is possible to proactively identify unusual patterns, ensuring security, efficiency, and better decision-making in real-world scenarios.

CHAPTER 17. AUTOMATED PIPELINES

Workflow automation in Machine Learning is essential to ensure efficiency, reproducibility, and scalability in data science projects. In Scikit-Learn, automated pipelines play a crucial role by organizing data preprocessing, feature engineering, and model training into a single execution flow. This approach eliminates the need to rewrite repetitive steps, reduces errors, and improves standardization.

Creating pipelines in Scikit-Learn allows all data transformations and modeling to be organized within a modular and reusable structure. This functionality is essential for building both simple models and complex production systems.

Components, Templates, and Metadata

The Scikit-Learn Pipeline follows a standardized structure composed of a sequence of steps, where each one represents a specific data transformation. These steps can include:

- **Data preprocessing**: Normalization, standardization, handling missing values.

- **Feature engineering**: Feature selection and extraction, categorical encoding.

- **Model training**: Application of the chosen Machine Learning algorithm.

- **Hyperparameter optimization**: Automatic search for the model's best parameters.

The Pipeline is structured using the **Pipeline** class, which encapsulates all workflow stages. Each step receives an identifier name and a corresponding transformation.

General structure of a pipeline in Scikit-Learn:

python

```python
from sklearn.pipeline import Pipeline
from sklearn.preprocessing import StandardScaler
from sklearn.ensemble import RandomForestClassifier

# Defining the pipeline
pipeline = Pipeline([
    ('normalization', StandardScaler()),  # Preprocessing step
    ('model', RandomForestClassifier(n_estimators=100,
random_state=42))  # Machine Learning model
])

# Applying the pipeline to a dataset
pipeline.fit(X_train, y_train)
predictions = pipeline.predict(X_test)
```

This approach ensures that all steps are correctly applied to any new dataset, guaranteeing consistency and minimizing human errors.

Structural Directives and Attributes

Scikit-Learn pipelines follow a clear structure, ensuring modularity and organization. Their main attributes include:

- **steps**: List of pipeline steps.

- **named_steps**: Dictionary with the step names, facilitating individual access.

- **fit(X, y)**: Fits all transformations and the final model to the data.

- **predict(X)**: Applies transformations and generates predictions with the trained model.

Practical example with feature extraction and modeling inside a pipeline:

python

```
from sklearn.decomposition import PCA
from sklearn.svm import SVC

# Creating a pipeline with dimensionality reduction and SVM model
pipeline = Pipeline([
    ('dimensionality_reduction', PCA(n_components=2)),
    ('model', SVC(kernel='linear'))
])

# Fitting the pipeline
pipeline.fit(X_train, y_train)

# Making predictions
y_pred = pipeline.predict(X_test)
```

Here, the data first passes through dimensionality reduction using PCA before training the SVM model.

Introduction to Creating and Using Pipelines in Scikit-Learn

Creating automated pipelines offers several benefits:

- **Modular organization**: All steps are defined in a cohesive and sequential flow.

- **Reproducibility**: Ensures that the same preprocessing is always applied consistently.

- **Reduction of redundant code**: Avoids manually reapplying each transformation before model training.

- **Ease of optimization**: Pipelines can be combined with GridSearchCV for automated hyperparameter tuning.

Combining Pipelines with Cross-validation

Pipelines can be integrated with cross-validation to efficiently evaluate model performance.

python
```
from sklearn.model_selection import cross_val_score

# Executing cross-validation on the pipeline
scores = cross_val_score(pipeline, X, y, cv=5)
print("Pipeline average accuracy:", scores.mean())
```

Thus, all pipeline steps are correctly applied to each subset during cross-validation.

Hyperparameter Optimization inside a Pipeline

Another essential functionality of Scikit-Learn pipelines is their compatibility with GridSearchCV, allowing optimized hyperparameter searches.

python
```
from sklearn.model_selection import GridSearchCV
```

```python
# Defining the pipeline with an SVM model
pipeline = Pipeline([
    ('normalization', StandardScaler()),
    ('model', SVC())
])

# Defining the hyperparameter grid
parameters = {
    'model__C': [0.1, 1, 10],
    'model__kernel': ['linear', 'rbf']
}

# Optimization with GridSearchCV
grid_search = GridSearchCV(pipeline, parameters, cv=5)
grid_search.fit(X_train, y_train)

# Best hyperparameter combination found
print("Best parameters:", grid_search.best_params_)
```

Using GridSearchCV inside the pipeline eliminates data leakage risks and ensures that all transformations are correctly applied during the optimization process.

Common Errors and Recommended Solutions

Error: "Pipeline object has no attribute predict"
Occurs when trying to predict before fitting the pipeline.
Recommended Solution: Ensure that the .fit(X, y) method is executed before calling .predict(X).

python
```python
pipeline.fit(X_train, y_train)
predictions = pipeline.predict(X_test)
```

Error: "GridSearchCV not recognizing pipeline parameters"
If GridSearchCV does not recognize the pipeline parameters, it is likely that the step names were incorrectly specified.
Recommended Solution: Always use step_name__parameter_name to reference hyperparameters inside the pipeline.

python
```
parameters = {
    'model__C': [0.1, 1, 10]  # Correct name format
}
```

Error: Data Leakage during cross-validation
Data leakage occurs when transformations like normalization are applied before splitting the data into train and test.
Recommended Solution: Always encapsulate transformations within the pipeline so that each step is applied only to training data inside the cross-validation.

Best Practices and Real Applications

- Always encapsulate all transformations in the pipeline, including preprocessing, feature selection, and modeling.

- Use GridSearchCV to optimize hyperparameters without risking data leakage.

- Use pipelines for production implementation, ensuring all steps are replicable and standardized.

Real-world applications of automated pipelines include:

- Large-scale predictive models, ensuring that new data is properly treated before predictions.

- Recommendation systems, optimizing feature selection and transformation before model usage.

- Financial fraud classification, where multiple preprocessing steps are necessary to handle raw data.

The use of automated pipelines in Scikit-Learn significantly improves workflow efficiency and organization in Machine Learning. By correctly applying this approach, it is possible to build robust, modular, and reproducible solutions, ensuring that all process steps are executed consistently. Integrating pipelines with cross-validation and hyperparameter optimization raises the modeling level, allowing Machine Learning projects to be scalable and reliable in production environments.

CHAPTER 18. DEPLOYING SCIKIT-LEARN MODELS

The deployment of Machine Learning models is the stage that transforms an analytical solution developed in a development environment into a system ready for use in production. This process involves exporting the trained model, integrating it with applications, and making it available to users or external systems. Scikit-Learn offers several efficient ways to save, load, and implement models, ensuring scalability and reproducibility.

The choice of deployment approach depends on the execution environment. Models can be served via web APIs, embedded in local applications, or integrated with embedded and cloud systems. The use of tools like Flask, FastAPI, and Docker allows operationalizing models efficiently and scalably.

Components, Templates, and Metadata

Deploying a trained model in Scikit-Learn follows a modular structure, ensuring that all steps of the Machine Learning pipeline are preserved in the production environment. The main components involved in deployment include:

- **Model serialization**: Saving and loading the trained model using joblib or pickle.

- **Serving via API**: Creating an interface to receive data and return predictions.

- **Monitoring and updating**: Implementing mechanisms to

track model performance in production.

To ensure efficiency and reproducibility, the model must be saved and reused correctly. Scikit-Learn facilitates this process through joblib, which preserves complex objects like models and pipelines.

Saving and Loading Models with joblib

python

```python
from sklearn.ensemble import RandomForestClassifier
from sklearn.datasets import load_iris
from sklearn.model_selection import train_test_split
import joblib

# Loading the data
data = load_iris()
X_train, X_test, y_train, y_test = train_test_split(data.data,
data.target, test_size=0.2, random_state=42)

# Training the model
model = RandomForestClassifier(n_estimators=100)
model.fit(X_train, y_train)

# Saving the trained model
joblib.dump(model, 'model_rf.pkl')

# Loading the saved model
loaded_model = joblib.load('model_rf.pkl')

# Making predictions with the loaded model
predictions = loaded_model.predict(X_test)
print("Predictions:", predictions)
```

This process ensures that the trained model can be reused without retraining, optimizing performance in production.

Structural Directives and Attributes

The deployment structure must guarantee modularity and organization. The main components and attributes include:

- **Serialized models (.pkl or .joblib)**: Files containing trained models for future use.

- **APIs for consumption**: HTTP interfaces to allow external applications to send data and receive predictions.

- **Deployment pipeline**: Strategies to monitor and update models in production without interruptions.

Deployment can be performed in different ways, depending on the system's context and needs:

- **Local deployment**: The model is loaded directly into a software or Python script for internal use.

- **Deployment via API**: The model is made available for remote access through an HTTP server.

- **Containerized deployment**: The model is packaged in an isolated environment, such as Docker, facilitating scalability.

Introduction to Model Deployment in Production Environments

Deploying a model must follow best practices to ensure stability and security. Creating an API to serve predictions is one of the most used approaches to make models accessible to external systems.

Creating a Machine Learning API with Flask

python

```python
from flask import Flask, request, jsonify
import joblib
import numpy as np

# Loading the trained model
model = joblib.load("model_rf.pkl")

# Creating the Flask application
app = Flask(__name__)

# Endpoint for predictions
@app.route('/predict', methods=['POST'])
def predict():
    data = request.get_json()
    input_data = np.array(data['values']).reshape(1, -1)
    prediction = model.predict(input_data)
    return jsonify({'prediction': int(prediction[0])})

# Running the API
if __name__ == '__main__':
    app.run(port=5000, debug=True)
```

This code creates a local HTTP service that receives JSON data, executes predictions, and returns the result. The model can be accessed by any client application via HTTP requests.

Implementing a More Efficient API with FastAPI

While Flask is a popular option, FastAPI is a more efficient and modern alternative for creating Machine Learning APIs with better performance.

python
```
from fastapi import FastAPI
import joblib
import numpy as np

# Loading the trained model
model = joblib.load("model_rf.pkl")

# Creating the FastAPI application
app = FastAPI()

# Endpoint for predictions
@app.post("/predict/")
def predict(data: dict):
    input_data = np.array(data['values']).reshape(1, -1)
    prediction = model.predict(input_data)
    return {"prediction": int(prediction[0])}
```

FastAPI is faster than Flask and allows automatic input validation, making it recommended for large-scale systems.

Packaging the Model with

Docker for Scalable Deployment

Using Docker ensures that the execution environment is consistent and replicable, eliminating compatibility problems between systems.

Dockerfile for packaging the API:

dockerfile
```
FROM python:3.9
WORKDIR /app
```

```
COPY . /app
RUN pip install -r requirements.txt
CMD ["python", "api.py"]
```

To run the API inside the container:

sh

```
docker build -t ml_api .
docker run -p 5000:5000 ml_api
```

This ensures that the model is ready for production without additional configuration.

Common Errors and Recommended Solutions

Error: "ModuleNotFoundError: No module named 'sklearn'"
Occurs when trying to load a trained model in an environment without the necessary libraries.
Recommended Solution: Ensure the execution environment contains all dependencies and use:

sh

```
pip install -r requirements.txt
```

before running the code.

Error: "Flask app not running on expected port"
Occurs if another application is already using the configured port.
Recommended Solution: Modify the Flask application port:

python

```
app.run(port=8000)
```

Error: Model trained on a different version of Scikit-Learn
If a model trained in an old version of Scikit-Learn is loaded into

a newer version, compatibility errors may arise.

Recommended Solution: Always save the version used along with the model:

sh
```
pip freeze > requirements.txt
```

allowing the exact environment to be recreated later.

Best Practices and Real Applications

- Always version trained models to facilitate rollback in case of problems.

- Monitor model performance in production, identifying possible accuracy drops over time.

- Automate model revalidation, ensuring that new versions are tested before replacement.

Real-world applications of Machine Learning model deployment include:

- **Financial fraud detection:** Models serving real-time predictions for banking transactions.

- **Virtual assistants and chatbots**: Machine Learning APIs automatically analyzing and processing text.

- **Predictive maintenance**: Systems analyzing industrial sensor data to predict equipment failures.

Deploying Machine Learning models with Scikit-Learn allows transforming analytical solutions into scalable and efficient operational systems. Using serialization techniques, web APIs, and containers, it is possible to guarantee model reproducibility and stability. By following best practices for implementation and monitoring, the transition from development to production becomes efficient, enabling the practical use of Machine Learning solutions in real-time environments.

CHAPTER 19. WORKING WITH IMBALANCED DATA

Class imbalance is a common problem in Machine Learning, especially in applications where some classes are significantly more frequent than others. Examples include fraud detection, medical diagnostics, and cybersecurity, where positive events (fraud, disease, or attack) are much less frequent than negative events.

Machine Learning models, when trained on imbalanced data, can develop a bias toward the majority class, reducing their ability to correctly identify minority class cases. To mitigate this problem, several techniques are used to adjust class distribution and improve prediction quality.

Components, Templates, and Metadata

When working with imbalanced data, it is essential to use strategies to balance class distribution and avoid model bias. The main approaches include:

- **Data Resampling**: Techniques like oversampling and undersampling to adjust class proportions.

- **Use of Appropriate Metrics**: Accuracy can be misleading on imbalanced datasets. Metrics like F1-score, recall, and precision are more suitable.

- **Adjusting Class Weights**: Modifying model hyperparameters to assign greater weight to underrepresented classes.

- **Using Specialized Algorithms**: Models like Balanced Random Forest and SMOTEBoost are designed to handle class imbalance.

Scikit-Learn supports all these techniques, allowing model training to properly account for uneven class distributions.

Structural Directives and Attributes

The main methods available to handle imbalanced data in Scikit-Learn include:

Oversampling (increasing the minority class):

- **SMOTE (Synthetic Minority Over-sampling Technique)**: Generates new synthetic examples for the minority class.

- **ADASYN (Adaptive Synthetic Sampling)**: Similar to SMOTE but focuses on harder-to-learn examples.

Undersampling (reducing the majority class):

- **Random Undersampling**: Randomly removes examples from the majority class to balance distribution.

- **NearMiss**: Selects majority class examples closest to the minority class.

Adjusting class weights in the model:

- Many algorithms allow setting class weights to minimize the impact of imbalance.

- **class_weight='balanced'** parameter available in algorithms like RandomForestClassifier and LogisticRegression.

Code to analyze class distribution:

python
```
import numpy as np
from collections import Counter
from sklearn.datasets import make_classification

# Creating an imbalanced dataset
X, y = make_classification(n_classes=2, class_sep=2,
weights=[0.90, 0.10],
                    n_informative=3, n_redundant=1, flip_y=0,
n_features=5,
                    n_clusters_per_class=1, n_samples=1000,
random_state=42)

# Displaying class distribution
print("Original class distribution:", Counter(y))
```

This code creates an imbalanced dataset, where 90% of the data belongs to the majority class and only 10% belongs to the minority class.

Introduction to Techniques
for Handling Imbalanced Data

When dealing with imbalanced data, it is necessary to choose the correct approach to prevent the model from becoming biased. Scikit-Learn provides various tools to balance data before training.

Oversampling with SMOTE

SMOTE creates synthetic examples for the minority class to balance the distribution.

python

```
from imblearn.over_sampling import SMOTE

# Applying SMOTE to balance the data
smote = SMOTE(sampling_strategy=0.5, random_state=42)
X_res, y_res = smote.fit_resample(X, y)

# Displaying the new class distribution
print("Class distribution after SMOTE:", Counter(y_res))
```

SMOTE is useful when there are few examples of the minority class and increases example diversity.

Undersampling with Random Undersampling

If the majority class is overrepresented, undersampling can be used to reduce its quantity.

python
```
from imblearn.under_sampling import RandomUnderSampler

# Applying Random Undersampling
undersample = RandomUnderSampler(sampling_strategy=0.5,
random_state=42)
X_res, y_res = undersample.fit_resample(X, y)

# Displaying the new class distribution
print("Class distribution after undersampling:", Counter(y_res))
```

Undersampling reduces the number of majority class examples, ensuring the model does not focus excessively on it.

Using class_weight during model training

Algorithms like RandomForestClassifier, LogisticRegression, and SVM allow setting class weights to compensate for imbalance.

python
```
from sklearn.ensemble import RandomForestClassifier
from sklearn.model_selection import train_test_split
from sklearn.metrics import classification_report

# Splitting the data
X_train, X_test, y_train, y_test = train_test_split(X, y,
test_size=0.2, random_state=42)

# Creating model with class weight adjustment
model = RandomForestClassifier(class_weight="balanced",
random_state=42)
model.fit(X_train, y_train)

# Predicting and evaluating
y_pred = model.predict(X_test)
print(classification_report(y_test, y_pred))
```

Adjusting **class_weight** causes the model to assign greater importance to underrepresented classes, improving prediction capability.

Common Errors and Recommended Solutions

Error: "ValueError: Expected 2D array, got 1D array instead"
Occurs when data format is incorrect when using methods like fit_resample().
Recommended Solution: Ensure data is properly structured before applying SMOTE or undersampling.

python
```
X_res, y_res = smote.fit_resample(X.reshape(-1, 1), y)
```

Error: Model still favors the majority class

Even after balancing, the model may continue predicting mostly the majority class.
Recommended Solutions:

- Use an appropriate metric: Accuracy is unreliable for imbalanced data. Use F1-score and recall.

- Try different balancing techniques, such as combining SMOTE with class_weight='balanced'.

python
```
from sklearn.metrics import f1_score
f1 = f1_score(y_test, y_pred)
print("F1-score:", f1)
```

Error: Overfitting when using SMOTE
SMOTE can generate synthetic samples too similar to each other, leading to overfitting.
Recommended Solution: Reduce the oversampling rate or try ADASYN, which distributes samples adaptively.

python
```
from imblearn.over_sampling import ADASYN
adasyn = ADASYN(sampling_strategy=0.5, random_state=42)
X_res, y_res = adasyn.fit_resample(X, y)
```

Best Practices and Real Applications

- **Choose the balancing technique based on dataset size:**

  o If there is a lot of data available, undersampling can

be efficient.

- o   If there is little data, SMOTE or ADASYN are more appropriate.

- **Use appropriate metrics**: Prefer F1-score, recall, and AUC-ROC instead of just accuracy.

- **Avoid excessive balancing**: Creating too many synthetic examples can lead to a model that does not generalize well.

Real-world applications of data balancing:

- **Financial fraud detection**: Ensuring that fraud is correctly identified without generating too many false positives.

- **Medical diagnosis**: Improving the identification of rare diseases without compromising model reliability.

- **Cybersecurity analysis**: Detecting anomalous activities in networks without overfitting on normal data.

Working with imbalanced data is essential to ensure that Machine Learning models are accurate and fair. Techniques like SMOTE, undersampling, and weight adjustments allow balancing class distribution and improving the model's ability to correctly identify rare events. By applying these strategies efficiently, it is possible to create robust and reliable solutions for different practical problems.

CHAPTER 20. INTEGRATION WITH OTHER LIBRARIES

Scikit-Learn is one of the most widely used libraries for Machine Learning in Python, but its isolated use is rarely enough to develop complete solutions. Integration with auxiliary libraries such as Pandas, NumPy, and Matplotlib is essential for data manipulation, visualization, and result analysis. These tools complement Machine Learning algorithms, enabling more efficient and optimized workflows.

Integration with Pandas facilitates structured dataset manipulation, while Matplotlib and Seaborn are indispensable for visual analysis and model interpretation. NumPy ensures efficient mathematical operations and compatibility with Scikit-Learn. Combined, these libraries enable the development of robust data science pipelines.

Components, Templates, and Metadata

The integration of Scikit-Learn with other libraries follows a modular structure. Each tool plays a fundamental role:

- **Pandas**: Data manipulation and cleaning.

- **NumPy**: Efficient mathematical operations and array compatibility.

- **Matplotlib and Seaborn**: Graphical visualization and exploratory analysis.

- **SciPy**: Support for advanced statistics and optimization.

- **Joblib**: Fast model serialization and loading.

These libraries ensure greater flexibility and performance when working with Machine Learning models.

Structural Directives and Attributes

Using Pandas and NumPy in Scikit-Learn is essential for efficient data handling. Pandas represents datasets as DataFrames, while NumPy facilitates matrix operations needed for model training.

Loading data with Pandas:

python
```
import pandas as pd

# Loading a CSV dataset
data = pd.read_csv("data.csv")

# Viewing the first rows
print(data.head())
```

Converting a DataFrame to NumPy:

Scikit-Learn works directly with NumPy arrays. To integrate Pandas with models, DataFrames must be properly converted.

python
```
import numpy as np

# Converting DataFrame to NumPy array
X = data.drop(columns=["target"]).values
y = data["target"].values
```

This process ensures data compatibility with Scikit-Learn algorithms.

Integration with Matplotlib for visualization:

Visualizing data is essential for understanding patterns and evaluating model performance.

python

```
import matplotlib.pyplot as plt

# Creating a histogram to analyze the distribution of a variable
plt.hist(data["age"], bins=30, color='blue', edgecolor='black')
plt.xlabel("Age")
plt.ylabel("Frequency")
plt.title("Age Distribution")
plt.show()
```

Matplotlib integration with Pandas allows for visual exploration of the data before training.

Introduction to Integration with Libraries like Pandas and Matplotlib

Integration between Scikit-Learn, Pandas, and Matplotlib ensures an efficient workflow for data analysis, training, and evaluation of Machine Learning models.

Data preprocessing with Pandas:

Before training a model, data must be cleaned and transformed. Pandas offers functionalities to handle missing values, normalize columns, and create new variables.

python

```
# Removing missing values
data = data.dropna()

# Normalizing values between 0 and 1
data["age"] = (data["age"] - data["age"].min()) / (data["age"].max()
- data["age"].min())
```

These transformations ensure that the model receives well-prepared data for training.

Using Seaborn for visual analysis:

Seaborn is an extension of Matplotlib that facilitates the creation of informative graphics.

python
```python
import seaborn as sns

# Creating a scatter plot between two variables
sns.scatterplot(x=data["salary"], y=data["age"],
hue=data["target"])
plt.title("Relationship between Salary and Age")
plt.show()
```

Visualization with Seaborn helps identify patterns and relationships in the data.

Complete Integration Pipeline

Below is an example of a complete workflow, from data loading to model training with Pandas and Scikit-Learn.

python
```python
from sklearn.model_selection import train_test_split
from sklearn.ensemble import RandomForestClassifier
from sklearn.metrics import classification_report

# Loading the data
data = pd.read_csv("data.csv")

# Separating independent variables and target
X = data.drop(columns=["target"])
```

```
y = data["target"]

# Splitting data into training and testing
X_train, X_test, y_train, y_test = train_test_split(X, y,
test_size=0.2, random_state=42)

# Creating and training the model
model = RandomForestClassifier(n_estimators=100)
model.fit(X_train, y_train)

# Making predictions
y_pred = model.predict(X_test)

# Evaluating performance
print(classification_report(y_test, y_pred))
```

This code demonstrates a complete pipeline integrating Pandas, Scikit-Learn, and evaluation metrics.

Common Errors and Recommended Solutions

Error: "ValueError: Expected 2D array, got 1D array instead"
Occurs when trying to pass a Pandas Series to a Scikit-Learn model.
Recommended Solution: Use .values.reshape(-1, 1) to ensure the data is two-dimensional.

python
```
X = data["age"].values.reshape(-1, 1)
```

Error: "KeyError: 'target'" when loading data
Occurs when the specified column does not exist in the DataFrame.
Recommended Solution: Check column names with

data.columns.

Error: Plot not displaying correctly in Matplotlib
If the plot does not display properly, it may be necessary to use
plt.show() at the end.
Recommended Solution:

python
```
plt.show()
```

Best Practices and Real Applications

- Always normalize data before training to ensure models handle different scales well.

- Use exploratory graphics to check data quality and identify hidden patterns.

- Optimize computational efficiency by using NumPy for vectorized operations whenever possible.

Real-world applications of Scikit-Learn integration with Pandas and Matplotlib:

- **Financial analysis**: Credit models integrated with Pandas for risk analysis and prediction.

- **Medical diagnostics**: Disease classification using Machine Learning and pattern visualization with Seaborn.

- **Network monitoring**: Anomaly detection in traffic logs with Pandas and Machine Learning.

The integration of Scikit-Learn with Pandas, Matplotlib, and other libraries is essential for an efficient workflow in Machine Learning. Using these tools together, it is possible to process data in a structured way, visualize relevant patterns, and build more accurate predictive models. Mastery of these integrations enables the development of more robust, scalable, and applicable Machine Learning solutions across different fields of knowledge.

CHAPTER 21. AUTOMATION AND AUTOML

The automation of processes in Machine Learning has become essential to optimize workflows and improve efficiency in building predictive models. AutoML (Automated Machine Learning) is an approach that automates tasks such as model selection, hyperparameter tuning, and feature engineering, reducing experimentation time and enhancing solution performance. Scikit-Learn, together with specialized tools like Auto-sklearn, enables the integration of automation into model development without compromising result quality.

Components, Templates, and Metadata

Automation in Machine Learning is based on three main pillars:

- **Automatic model selection**: Different algorithms are tested to find the best option for the data.

- **Hyperparameter tuning**: Automatic search for the ideal parameters to maximize model performance.

- **Feature engineering**: Identification and transformation of the most relevant variables for prediction.

The Auto-sklearn library implements these principles, using Bayesian optimization and advanced techniques to automatically find the best model.

Structural Directives and Attributes

The main attributes of automation in AutoML involve configuring optimized pipelines and using cross-validation to ensure robustness.

- **Auto-sklearn**: A Scikit-Learn-based implementation that tests different combinations of algorithms and hyperparameters automatically.

- **TPOT**: A tool that uses genetic algorithms to find the best Machine Learning pipeline.

- **H2O AutoML**: A powerful platform for large-scale AutoML.

The integration of these frameworks with Scikit-Learn facilitates automation without the need for complex manual adjustments.

Introduction to AutoML Tools with Scikit-Learn (Auto-sklearn, for example)

Auto-sklearn is one of the most efficient tools for Machine Learning automation based on Scikit-Learn. It automatically searches for models and hyperparameters, ensuring that the best combination is used for a specific dataset.

Installing Auto-sklearn:

python
```
pip install auto-sklearn
```

Using Auto-sklearn to Find the Best Model:

python
```
import autosklearn.classification
from sklearn.model_selection import train_test_split
from sklearn.datasets import load_digits
from sklearn.metrics import accuracy_score
```

```
# Loading a dataset
data = load_digits()
X_train, X_test, y_train, y_test = train_test_split(data.data,
data.target, test_size=0.2, random_state=42)

# Creating the AutoML classifier
automl_model =
autosklearn.classification.AutoSklearnClassifier(time_left_for_
this_task=300, per_run_time_limit=30)

# Automatically fitting the model
automl_model.fit(X_train, y_train)

# Making predictions
y_pred = automl_model.predict(X_test)

# Evaluating performance
print("AutoML model accuracy:", accuracy_score(y_test,
y_pred))
```

The code above runs AutoML for 5 minutes, testing different models and returning the best configuration found.

Automation with TPOT

TPOT (Tree-based Pipeline Optimization Tool) uses genetic algorithms to optimize Machine Learning models.

python
```
from tpot import TPOTClassifier

# Creating the TPOT classifier
tpot_model = TPOTClassifier(generations=5,
population_size=20, verbosity=2)
```

```python
# Fitting the model
tpot_model.fit(X_train, y_train)

# Making predictions
y_pred = tpot_model.predict(X_test)

# Evaluating performance
print("TPOT accuracy:", accuracy_score(y_test, y_pred))
```

TPOT generates an optimized pipeline and provides the corresponding Python code for future use.

Automation with H2O AutoML

H2O AutoML is one of the most powerful solutions for large-scale Machine Learning automation. It quickly tests models and is highly efficient for large datasets.

```python
import h2o
from h2o.automl import H2OAutoML

# Initializing H2O
h2o.init()

# Converting the data to H2O format
data_h2o = h2o.H2OFrame(data.data)
data_h2o["target"] = h2o.H2OFrame(data.target)

# Splitting the data
train, test = data_h2o.split_frame(ratios=[0.8])

# Creating AutoML
h2o_model = H2OAutoML(max_models=10, seed=42)
```

```
h2o_model.train(y="target", training_frame=train)

# Making predictions
predictions = h2o_model.predict(test)
print(predictions)
```

H2O AutoML tests several models and returns the best ones based on performance metrics.

Common Errors and Recommended Solutions

Error: Auto-sklearn requires SWIG
If an error related to SWIG occurs when installing Auto-sklearn, it means the dependency is not installed.
Recommended Solution: Install SWIG before trying to install Auto-sklearn.

```sh
sudo apt install swig
pip install auto-sklearn
```

Error: Auto-sklearn does not support large datasets
Auto-sklearn can be slow for large datasets.
Recommended Solution: Use random sampling to reduce the data size before running AutoML.

```python
X_sample, _, y_sample, _ = train_test_split(X, y,
train_size=10000, random_state=42)
```

Error: TPOT takes too long to train
TPOT can take hours to find the best pipeline depending on the number of generations configured.
Recommended Solution: Reduce generations and population_size to speed up execution.

```python
```

```
tpot_model = TPOTClassifier(generations=2,
population_size=10)
```

Error: H2O AutoML consumes too much memory
H2O can use a large amount of RAM when processing large volumes of data.
Recommended Solution: Set a limit for the number of models and adjust the maximum available memory.

python
```
h2o.init(max_mem_size="4G")
h2o_model = H2OAutoML(max_models=5, seed=42)
```

Best Practices and Real Applications

- Use AutoML to quickly explore different models without manually testing many combinations.

- Adjust execution time to avoid excessive resource consumption.

- Interpret generated models by checking which algorithms and hyperparameters were selected.

- Integrate AutoML with APIs and deployment systems for production applications.

Real-world Applications of AutoML:

- **Bank fraud detection**: Automatically testing different algorithms to find the most efficient one.

- **Medical classification**: Automatically tuning models for disease diagnosis.

- **Marketing campaign optimization**: Automatically

identifying behavioral patterns.

Automation with AutoML in Scikit-Learn is a powerful approach to quickly find the best combinations of algorithms and hyperparameters without manual intervention. Tools like Auto-sklearn, TPOT, and H2O AutoML allow efficient model optimization, reducing development time and improving predictive performance. By correctly applying these techniques, it is possible to create scalable and high-performance solutions for a wide range of real-world applications.

CHAPTER 22. MODEL INTERPRETATION (EXPLAINABILITY)

Model interpretability in Machine Learning has become a fundamental requirement in various applications, especially in sectors such as healthcare, finance, and law. With the advancement of complex models like neural networks and ensembles, the need to understand how and why a model makes decisions has become critical. Techniques such as SHAP (SHapley Additive Explanations) and LIME (Local Interpretable Model-agnostic Explanations) offer solutions to make predictive models more transparent and trustworthy.

The ability to interpret a model not only improves its reliability but also enables the identification of biases, systemic errors, and overall performance improvements.

Components, Templates, and Metadata

Model interpretability can be divided into three main approaches:

- **Global interpretation**: Understanding the overall logic and decision structure of the model.

- **Local interpretation**: Analyzing the reasons behind a specific prediction.

- **Feature Importance**: Measuring the impact of each

variable on the final outcome.

The SHAP library is based on Shapley value theory to distribute feature importance consistently and explainably. LIME creates small perturbations in input data to analyze how the model responds, generating understandable local explanations.

Structural Directives and Attributes

The main attributes of interpretability techniques include:

- **Global Feature Importance**: Determines which variables have the greatest overall impact on the model.

- **Local Explanations**: Explains individual predictions, allowing users to understand specific decisions.

- **Model-agnostic and model-specific techniques**: Some techniques are applicable to any model, while others are specific to certain types of algorithms.

Implementing these approaches allows evaluating model reliability and identifying potential ethical violations, undesirable biases, and predictive inconsistencies.

Introduction to SHAP, LIME, and Other Interpretability Techniques

Installing the required libraries:

python
```
pip install shap lime
```

Using SHAP to Interpret Models

The SHAP library enables analyzing which variables most influence model predictions.

python

```
import shap
import xgboost
from sklearn.model_selection import train_test_split
from sklearn.datasets import load_boston

# Loading a dataset
data = load_boston()
X_train, X_test, y_train, y_test = train_test_split(data.data,
data.target, test_size=0.2, random_state=42)

# Training an XGBoost model
model = xgboost.XGBRegressor()
model.fit(X_train, y_train)

# Creating the SHAP explainer
explainer = shap.Explainer(model, X_train)
shap_values = explainer(X_test)

# Generating feature importance plot
shap.summary_plot(shap_values, X_test,
feature_names=data.feature_names)
```

SHAP calculates feature importance consistently, allowing for a clear explanation of predictions.

Local Interpretation with LIME

LIME generates understandable explanations by slightly modifying input data and observing how it affects model prediction.

python
```
import lime
import lime.lime_tabular
from sklearn.ensemble import RandomForestClassifier
```

```
from sklearn.datasets import load_iris

# Loading the dataset
data = load_iris()
X_train, X_test, y_train, y_test = train_test_split(data.data,
data.target, test_size=0.2, random_state=42)

# Training a Random Forest model
model = RandomForestClassifier(n_estimators=100)
model.fit(X_train, y_train)

# Creating the LIME explainer
explainer = lime.lime_tabular.LimeTabularExplainer(X_train,
feature_names=data.feature_names,
class_names=data.target_names, discretize_continuous=True)

# Explanation for a specific prediction
explanation = explainer.explain_instance(X_test[0],
model.predict_proba)
explanation.show_in_notebook()
```

LIME generates a visual explanation of predictions, making model outputs more understandable.

Comparison Between SHAP and LIME

- **SHAP** offers global and local explanations based on solid mathematical theory, making it more robust for complex models.

- **LIME** is more intuitive and easier to interpret, ideal for quickly explaining individual predictions.

Both approaches are complementary and can be used together for a more comprehensive view of model interpretability.

Common Errors and Recommended Solutions

Error: "SHAP requires a trained model"
SHAP needs the model to be trained before generating explanations.
Recommended Solution: Ensure the model has been fitted before calling Explainer().

python
```
model.fit(X_train, y_train)
explainer = shap.Explainer(model, X_train)
```

Error: "LIME requires discretized data"
LIME may not work correctly on continuous data without discretization.
Recommended Solution: Use discretize_continuous=True when initializing LimeTabularExplainer.

python
```
explainer = lime.lime_tabular.LimeTabularExplainer(X_train, discretize_continuous=True)
```

Error: Deep learning models not correctly interpreted
Complex models may require specific configurations for SHAP or LIME to work well.
Recommended Solution: For neural networks, use specific methods like Deep SHAP for better compatibility.

python
```
explainer = shap.DeepExplainer(deep_model, X_train)
```

Best Practices and Real Applications

- Use SHAP to understand complex models like XGBoost and neural networks, ensuring transparency in predictions.

- Apply LIME in systems that require quick and understandable explanations for end-users.

- Combine different techniques for a complete view of model interpretability.

- Avoid automated biases by evaluating which variables most impact predictions.

Real-world applications of model interpretability:

- **AI-assisted medical diagnosis**: Clear explanations allow doctors to trust predictive models.

- **Bank credit and financial scoring**: Regulators require clear justifications for approvals and rejections.

- **Fraud detection systems**: Transparency about why a transaction was flagged as suspicious.

- **Legal and compliance systems**: AI decisions must be auditable and explainable.

The interpretability of Machine Learning models is essential to ensure trust, transparency, and ethics in Artificial Intelligence. Techniques like SHAP and LIME enable understanding how models make decisions, helping both data scientists and end-users to comprehend results. Proper use of these tools allows optimizing model performance, reducing biases, and increasing the adoption of AI-based solutions.

CHAPTER 23. INTEGRATION WITH BIG DATA (SPARK & DASK)

Scikit-Learn is widely used for data analysis and Machine Learning on medium-sized datasets. However, when working with Big Data, the volume, velocity, and variety of the data require more scalable solutions. This is where tools like Apache Spark and Dask come in, enabling the processing of large volumes of data distributed across multiple nodes.

Combining Scikit-Learn with Spark and Dask allows training Machine Learning models at scale, leveraging parallel and distributed processing. This approach is essential for scenarios where the data is too large to fit into the RAM of a single computer.

Components, Templates, and Metadata

The integration between Scikit-Learn, Apache Spark, and Dask can be structured into three main approaches:

- **Distributed processing**: Splits large datasets into multiple partitions for parallel processing.

- **Scalable model training**: Allows training Machine Learning models without exhausting available memory.

- **Optimized Big Data pipelines**: Uses parallelism for preprocessing, hyperparameter tuning, and inference.

Apache Spark MLlib is a scalable alternative to Scikit-Learn, while Dask extends Scikit-Learn's functionality to support large data volumes without major code changes.

Structural Directives and Attributes

The main attributes of integrating Scikit-Learn with Spark and Dask include:

- **Efficient data distribution**: Processing occurs across distributed nodes, avoiding memory bottlenecks.

- **Scikit-Learn-compatible APIs**: Dask offers a framework similar to Scikit-Learn, facilitating code migration.

- **Training optimization**: Techniques like MapReduce and parallelism accelerate processing of large data volumes.

Using these tools allows for processing, transforming, and modeling massive datasets without compromising computational efficiency.

How to Combine Scikit-Learn with Big Data Tools

Using Dask to Extend Scikit-Learn

Dask-ML allows training Scikit-Learn models at scale, automatically splitting the data into smaller parts and distributing processing.

Installing Dask-ML:

sh
```
pip install dask-ml dask distributed
```

Training Scikit-Learn Models with Dask:

python
```
import dask.dataframe as dd
from dask_ml.model_selection import train_test_split
from dask_ml.linear_model import LogisticRegression
```

```
# Loading massive data as a Dask DataFrame
data = dd.read_csv("large_data.csv")

# Separating independent variables and target
X = data.drop(columns=["target"])
y = data["target"]

# Splitting the data in a distributed manner
X_train, X_test, y_train, y_test = train_test_split(X, y,
test_size=0.2, random_state=42)

# Creating and training a logistic regression model
model = LogisticRegression()
model.fit(X_train, y_train)

# Making predictions
y_pred = model.predict(X_test)
print(y_pred.compute())
```

Dask-ML allows models to be trained and tested without loading the entire dataset into memory.

Using Apache Spark for Scalable Machine Learning

Spark MLlib is a distributed Machine Learning library that allows model training on Big Data clusters.

Installing PySpark:

sh
```
pip install pyspark
```

Training a Model with Spark MLlib:

python

```
from pyspark.sql import SparkSession
from pyspark.ml.classification import LogisticRegression
from pyspark.ml.feature import VectorAssembler

# Creating a Spark session
spark =
SparkSession.builder.appName("BigDataML").getOrCreate()

# Loading massive data
data = spark.read.csv("large_data.csv", header=True,
inferSchema=True)

# Converting columns into a feature vector
assembler = VectorAssembler(inputCols=data.columns[:-1],
outputCol="features")
transformed_data = assembler.transform(data)

# Creating the model
model = LogisticRegression(featuresCol="features",
labelCol="target")

# Fitting the model to the distributed dataset
trained_model = model.fit(transformed_data)

# Making predictions
predictions = trained_model.transform(transformed_data)
predictions.select("features", "prediction").show()
```

Spark MLlib processes data across distributed clusters, allowing Machine Learning models to be trained on terabytes of data without compromising local RAM.

Common Errors and Recommended Solutions

Error: "MemoryError" when trying to load a large dataset into Pandas
Recommended Solution: Use Dask to process data in chunks without loading it entirely into memory.

python
```
import dask.dataframe as dd
data = dd.read_csv("large_data.csv")
```

Error: "Job aborted due to stage failure" in Apache Spark
This error occurs when there is a communication problem between cluster nodes.
Recommended Solution: Check Spark configuration and adjust allocated resources.

sh
```
spark-submit --executor-memory 4G --num-executors 5
```

Error: "Dask scheduler timeout"
If Dask becomes stuck, it may be a problem with the scheduler configuration.
Recommended Solution: Start the scheduler manually before running the code.

sh
```
dask-scheduler
```

Best Practices and Real Applications

- Always partition large datasets before processing to avoid excessive memory consumption.

- Use Dask for Scikit-Learn models when the data volume is too large to fit into memory.

- Employ Spark MLlib for Big Data scenarios across

distributed clusters.

- Monitor CPU and memory usage to optimize the performance of parallel processing.

Real-world Applications of Scikit-Learn Integration with Spark and Dask:

- **Large-scale financial analysis**: Processing millions of banking transactions to predict fraud.

- **Medical science**: Training models for diagnosis in large medical imaging datasets.

- **Social network Big Data**: Predictive modeling on massive user data.

- **Recommendation systems**: Processing millions of interactions for personalized content delivery.

Integrating Scikit-Learn with Big Data using Spark and Dask enables Machine Learning models to scale to massive datasets without compromising efficiency. While Dask provides a straightforward path to extend Scikit-Learn on local machines, Spark MLlib enables distributed training across large clusters. By applying these strategies, it is possible to build robust, scalable, and optimized solutions for real-world high-volume data scenarios.

CHAPTER 24. MLOPS AND CI/ CD FOR SCIKIT-LEARN MODELS

The integration of MLOps (Machine Learning Operations) with CI/CD (Continuous Integration/Continuous Deployment) for Machine Learning models enables an automated and efficient workflow to train, validate, deploy, and monitor predictive models. Scikit-Learn, being one of the most widely used libraries for machine learning, can be integrated into modern pipelines to ensure reproducibility, scalability, and automation.

Implementing MLOps and CI/CD reduces the need for manual interventions, facilitates updating models in production, and improves the reliability of Machine Learning systems.

Components, Templates, and Metadata

Implementing MLOps for Scikit-Learn models involves several structured steps, each serving a specific purpose within the Machine Learning lifecycle:

- **Automated training and validation**: Pipeline configuration to update models whenever new data is added.

- **Model version control**: Using tools like DVC (Data Version Control) to track model and dataset versions.

- **Automated deployment**: Implementing the model in REST APIs, Kubernetes, or cloud services.

- **Continuous monitoring**: Analyzing model performance

in production to detect data drifts and performance degradation.

Combining MLOps and CI/CD enables Machine Learning teams to deploy models reliably and at scale.

Structural Directives and Attributes

The main elements of automation in MLOps with Scikit-Learn include:

- **Data and model versioning**: Ensures traceability and avoids inconsistencies.

- **Automated pipeline**: Uses tools like GitHub Actions, Jenkins, and GitLab CI/CD for complete automation.

- **Unit testing and validation**: Implements automatic tests to ensure new models do not introduce performance regressions.

- **Continuous deployment**: Uses tools like Docker, Kubernetes, and FastAPI to ensure stable deployment.

The optimized structure ensures that models are always updated and operational without the need for manual processes.

Continuous Integration and

Continuous Delivery of Models

Continuous Integration (CI) and Continuous Delivery (CD) in Machine Learning differ from traditional software development because they involve dynamic data and models that need real-time monitoring.

Configuring a CI/CD Pipeline for Machine Learning

An efficient pipeline can be structured with the following steps:

- Data preprocessing and cleaning

- Model training and validation

- Model version storage

- Automated deployment

- Model performance monitoring

Below is an example of an automated pipeline using GitHub Actions and DVC for dataset and model versioning.

Configuring DVC for Model Versioning

DVC (Data Version Control) allows versioning datasets and models, ensuring reproducibility.

sh
```
pip install dvc
dvc init
dvc remote add myremote s3://my-dvc-bucket
```

Next, add model files for version control:

sh
```
dvc add model.pkl
git add model.pkl.dvc .gitignore
git commit -m "Initial model version"
git push origin main
```

CI/CD Pipeline for Automatic Retraining

Below is an example of GitHub Actions for a Machine Learning pipeline that automatically retrains the model when new data is added to the repository.

yaml

```yaml
name: ML Pipeline

on:
  push:
    branches:
      - main

jobs:
  train_model:
    runs-on: ubuntu-latest
    steps:
      - name: Checkout repository
        uses: actions/checkout@v2

      - name: Set up Python environment
        uses: actions/setup-python@v2
        with:
          python-version: '3.9'

      - name: Install dependencies
        run: |
          pip install -r requirements.txt
          pip install dvc

      - name: Pull data and train model
        run: |
          dvc pull
          python train.py
```

```
- name: Save trained model
  run: |
    dvc add model.pkl
    git add model.pkl.dvc
    git commit -m "Updated model"
    git push
    dvc push
```

This pipeline automatically:

- Pulls data from the DVC repository

- Retrains the model with new data

- Stores the latest model version

- Publishes the model to the repository

This approach ensures that whenever new data is available, the model is updated and deployed automatically.

Continuous Deployment with Docker and FastAPI

After training, the model can be deployed as a REST API using FastAPI and Docker.

python
```python
from fastapi import FastAPI
import pickle
import numpy as np

app = FastAPI()

# Loading the trained model
with open("model.pkl", "rb") as f:
```

```
   model = pickle.load(f)

@app.post("/predict/")
def predict(data: list):
   input_data = np.array(data).reshape(1, -1)
   prediction = model.predict(input_data)
   return {"prediction": prediction.tolist()}
```

Now, create a Dockerfile to deploy the API:

dockerfile
```
FROM python:3.9
WORKDIR /app
COPY . /app
RUN pip install fastapi uvicorn scikit-learn
CMD ["uvicorn", "api:app", "--host", "0.0.0.0", "--port", "8000"]
```

Building and running the container:

sh
```
docker build -t ml-api .
docker run -p 8000:8000 ml-api
```

The model is now accessible via REST API, facilitating integration with external applications.

Common Errors and Recommended Solutions

Error: "DVC storage quota exceeded"
Occurs when the data repository exceeds the storage limit.
Recommended Solution: Use a scalable storage service such as AWS S3, Google Cloud Storage, or Azure Blob Storage.

sh

```
dvc remote add myremote gs://my-dvc-bucket
```

Error: Model trained locally but not available in the API
The model might be saved in the wrong directory, preventing its import by the API.
Recommended Solution: Verify if the model is correctly saved in the working directory.

```python
import os
print(os.listdir("."))
```

Error: CI/CD failing when running the pipeline
If the pipeline execution fails, it may be a dependency or permissions issue.
Recommended Solution: Use pip freeze to list dependencies and ensure they are all in requirements.txt.

```sh
pip freeze > requirements.txt
```

Best Practices and Real Applications

- Use automated pipelines to ensure models are updated whenever new data is added.

- Implement unit tests to verify that the model does not introduce performance regressions.

- Monitor model performance in production to detect concept drifts and the need for retraining.

- Use model versioning with DVC to track changes and ensure reproducibility.

Real-world Applications of MLOps and CI/CD

- **Recommendation systems**: Continuous model updates for real-time personalization.

- **Bank fraud detection**: Automated training to quickly identify new threats.

- **Medical classification**: Automated deployment of models for AI-based diagnostics.

The integration of MLOps and CI/CD with Scikit-Learn allows Machine Learning models to be developed, versioned, tested, and deployed automatically, ensuring greater reliability and scalability. With well-structured pipelines, models can be kept up-to-date, reducing operational risks and improving the efficiency of AI applied across various sectors.

CHAPTER 25. ADVANCED TESTING AND DEBUGGING IN MACHINE LEARNING

Model validation in Machine Learning goes beyond simply evaluating performance metrics. To ensure that a model works reliably in different scenarios, it is essential to apply advanced testing, debugging, and profiling techniques. Scikit-Learn provides tools that allow verifying model robustness, identifying hidden errors, and optimizing Machine Learning pipelines.

Testing in Machine Learning involves different approaches, such as unit testing for auxiliary functions, performance validation with different datasets, and logical error debugging. Integrating debugging and profiling techniques enables a detailed analysis of model behavior, ensuring greater reliability and computational efficiency.

Components, Templates, and Metadata

Advanced testing and debugging in Machine Learning can be divided into three essential areas:

- **Unit testing for auxiliary functions and data preprocessing**

- **Model validation and error analysis**

- **Profiling and performance optimization**

Adopting these practices ensures that models maintain high accuracy and are robust against unexpected data variations.

Structural Directives and Attributes

The main attributes of advanced testing and debugging include:

- **Data integrity tests**: Verify the consistency of input data before training.

- **Model robustness tests**: Evaluate how a model behaves with different data distributions.

- **Debugging and error analysis**: Identify prediction failures and help adjust hyperparameters.

- **Pipeline performance profiling**: Optimize execution time and reduce memory consumption.

Implementing these practices increases model reliability and facilitates the correction of failures before deployment.

Testing Techniques, Debugging, and Profiling for Scikit-Learn Pipelines

Unit Testing for Auxiliary Functions

pytest is one of the most widely used tools for testing in Python and can be applied to auxiliary Machine Learning functions.

Installing pytest:

sh
```
pip install pytest
```

Creating a unit test for input data validation:

python

```
import pytest
import pandas as pd
from sklearn.preprocessing import StandardScaler

# Function that normalizes data
def normalize_data(df):
    scaler = StandardScaler()
    return scaler.fit_transform(df)

# Test to verify if the function handles missing values correctly
def test_normalize_data():
    df = pd.DataFrame({"column1": [10, 20, None, 40], "column2":
[1, 2, 3, 4]})
    with pytest.raises(ValueError):
        normalize_data(df)
```

The test verifies if the function raises an error when finding missing values, ensuring issues are addressed before model training.

Testing Model Robustness

Structured tests can verify if a model maintains performance under different conditions.

python
```
from sklearn.ensemble import RandomForestClassifier
from sklearn.datasets import make_classification
from sklearn.model_selection import train_test_split
from sklearn.metrics import accuracy_score
import numpy as np

# Generating synthetic test data
X, y = make_classification(n_samples=1000, n_features=20,
random_state=42)
```

```
X_train, X_test, y_train, y_test = train_test_split(X, y,
test_size=0.2, random_state=42)

# Creating and training the model
model = RandomForestClassifier(n_estimators=100)
model.fit(X_train, y_train)

# Testing robustness with noisy data
X_test_noise = X_test + np.random.normal(0, 0.5, X_test.shape)
y_pred = model.predict(X_test_noise)

# Verifying if accuracy remains acceptable
assert accuracy_score(y_test, y_pred) > 0.7, "Model lost too
much precision on noisy data"
```

This test ensures the model maintains its accuracy even when the data contains noise, essential for real-world applications.

Debugging Errors with SHAP and

Analyzing Unexpected Predictions

The SHAP library can help understand why a model makes certain errors.

python
```
import shap

explainer = shap.Explainer(model, X_train)
shap_values = explainer(X_test)

# Visualizing variable importance for a wrong prediction
shap.plots.waterfall(shap_values[0])
```

This approach identifies patterns in incorrect predictions and adjusts the model to reduce errors.

Profiling and Optimizing Pipelines

Profiling allows analyzing pipeline performance and identifying bottlenecks that affect model efficiency.

Using cProfile to Analyze Pipeline Performance:

sh
```
python -m cProfile -s time train.py
```

This analysis provides information about which parts of the code consume the most time, enabling optimizations.

Using memory_profiler to Identify Memory Consumption:

sh
```
pip install memory_profiler
```

python
```
from memory_profiler import profile

@profile
def train_model():
    model = RandomForestClassifier(n_estimators=100)
    model.fit(X_train, y_train)

train_model()
```

With memory_profiler, it is possible to optimize the model's memory consumption, avoiding waste of computational resources.

Common Errors and Recommended Solutions

Error: "AssertionError: Model lost too much precision on noisy

data"
Indicates that the model is not robust enough to handle noisy data.
Recommended Solution: Adjust model hyperparameters to make it more resistant.

python
```
model           =           RandomForestClassifier(n_estimators=200,
max_depth=10)
```

Error: "MemoryError" when training large models
Occurs when memory consumption exceeds availability.
Recommended Solution: Use Dask to process data in chunks and avoid overload.

python
```
import dask.dataframe as dd
data = dd.read_csv("large_data.csv")
```

Error: "Tests failing due to NaN values"
Occurs when a unit test fails due to missing values in the data.
Recommended Solution: Fill missing values before applying tests.

python
```
df = df.fillna(df.mean())
```

Best Practices and Real Applications

- Test every stage of the Machine Learning pipeline to avoid failures in production.

- Use profiling tools to optimize model execution time and memory usage.

- Automate tests using pytest and integrate them into CI/ CD pipelines.

- Analyze errors with SHAP to identify patterns in incorrect predictions.

Real-world Applications of Testing and Debugging in Machine Learning

- **Medical diagnostic model validation**: Ensures that AI does not make critical mistakes in diagnoses.

- **Bank fraud detection**: Automated testing helps avoid false positives in predictive models.

- **Credit classification**: Error debugging improves the accuracy of models used by banks.

Implementing advanced testing, debugging, and profiling in Scikit-Learn is essential to ensure that Machine Learning models are accurate, efficient, and robust against failures. With well-structured practices, it is possible to avoid unexpected errors, improve model reliability, and ensure safe deployment in real-world applications.

FINAL CONCLUSION

The learning journey covered throughout this book reflects the broad relevance of Scikit-Learn as an essential pillar in the formation of any professional working in data science. Understanding the theory and practice behind Machine Learning algorithms goes far beyond simple ready-made codes. It is about building a solid knowledge base that allows the creation of robust, scalable, and secure solutions. It is precisely by mastering the versatility of Scikit-Learn that opportunities arise to apply innovative ideas and conduct complex data analyses with a high level of precision.

The first stage, presented in Chapter 1, explained what Scikit-Learn is and offered an overview of its history and evolution. It also clarified the differences between this library and other Machine Learning solutions, highlighting the component-based architecture as one of the framework's great strengths. This starting point lays the foundation for how Scikit-Learn internally organizes its classes, estimators, and transformers, a structure that permeates all subsequent stages of the book.

In Chapter 2, the focus was on installing and configuring the environment, covering everything from acquiring Python and Scikit-Learn itself to creating the first Machine Learning project. It also explained the basic project structure, showing how using a well-organized directory and the requirements.txt file ensures reproducibility. This initial approach facilitates collaboration with other developers and avoids dependency issues across different machines. Additionally, it showed how to test the installation to ensure that all libraries were correctly configured.

Moving forward, Chapter 3 addressed the structure and fundamental concepts of Scikit-Learn, including components, templates, and metadata. A key part was the introduction to Python and its role within Scikit-Learn, emphasizing that although the library is specialized in Machine Learning, it is always anchored in the pillars of the Python ecosystem. Structural guidelines and attributes were also discussed, pointing out common mistakes that beginners or those who do not follow the standards properly might make. This phase closed by illustrating the importance of maintaining clean and well-documented code, showing real-world applications that reflect the robustness of this approach.

Chapter 4 delved into working with estimators. It was a significant step in understanding how Scikit-Learn handles basic algorithms, from the simplest to the more sophisticated ones, always maintaining the standardized fit, predict, and score interface. This chapter highlighted that the uniformity of Scikit-Learn simplifies the learning curve and facilitates algorithm swapping, allowing quick testing of different options. The main errors and recommended solutions made the learning practical, helping to circumvent recurring issues in algorithm implementations.

Following this logical progression, Chapter 5 brought data preprocessing to the forefront, emphasizing the importance of correctly preparing data before feeding any model. Concepts like normalization, standardization, and handling missing values were deepened, demonstrating how preprocessing techniques can improve a model's overall performance. Examples showed how Scikit-Learn already offers ready-to-use transformers, greatly simplifying the adoption of these practices. The final advice reinforced the relevance of always verifying the integrity and homogeneity of variables before proceeding.

Chapter 6 presented the Feature Engineering process with

Scikit-Learn. At this stage, it was defined how to create and select the right variables (features) for a problem. It explained why feature engineering is fundamental to improving the predictive capacity of algorithms. Methods like PolynomialFeatures and OneHotEncoder were discussed, which expand the possibilities of data representation. The main message is clear: with good feature choices, models can capture more complex relationships and provide more accurate predictions.

Next, Chapter 7 dealt with regression models. This topic showed how to handle both linear and nonlinear relationships, exploring essential algorithms for continuous value problems, such as linear regression and polynomial regression. It also demonstrated how to make predictions and evaluate metrics like R^2, MAE, and MSE, allowing a deep understanding of how a model fits the data and what adjustments might be necessary to improve its predictive power. This refers to the need for regular testing and caution with possible extrapolations.

In Chapter 8, it was the turn of classification models. The reader could understand the functioning of algorithms like Logistic Regression, Decision Trees, Random Forest, and K-Nearest Neighbors for problems where the target variables are categories. With this introduction, it becomes clear that each method has its peculiarities, indicating that the ideal algorithm choice depends on both the data type and the project's objective. Tips on using accuracy, precision, recall, and F1-score were valuable for properly evaluating performance in scenarios with different demands.

Chapter 9 exposed the theme of model validation and evaluation. With an emphasis on cross-validation techniques, the reader could see how to mitigate overfitting, obtaining reliable estimates of a model's real performance. It was emphasized that measuring only accuracy can be misleading in many contexts, leading to a discussion of specific metrics that better meet different needs. The careful approach to this chapter leads to a solid understanding of how to conduct reproducible and reliable experiments.

Following the line of continuously improving the model, Chapter 10 revealed hyperparameter tuning, with explanations on how techniques like GridSearchCV and RandomizedSearchCV can help find optimal settings to maximize model performance. This process is especially relevant for complex algorithms or those with many parameters. Common errors were also mentioned, such as incorrect use of cross-validation or system overload when testing too many combinations. In the end, it was highlighted that hyperparameter tuning can significantly impact prediction quality but must be done carefully and without neglecting overfitting analysis.

In Chapter 11, ensemble methods came into play. Techniques like Random Forest and Gradient Boosting allow combining multiple models to obtain more robust predictions. The central idea is that each model, when combined, corrects the others' errors, resulting in superior overall performance. The chapter also covered the main settings of these methods and how to manage parameters like n_estimators and learning_rate. The great value of ensembles lies in their ability to handle complex data without excessive tuning.

Chapter 12 focused on Support Vector Machines (SVM), a powerful algorithm for classification and regression. The explanation covered from the concept of the optimal hyperplane to the discussion of linear and nonlinear kernels, such as RBF and polynomial, which extend SVM's capabilities. Frequent problems were clarified, such as choosing the parameter C or gamma. The chapter also drew a parallel on how SVM differs from other algorithms in terms of robustness against noise or high dimensionality.

In Chapter 13, neural networks with MLPClassifier received special attention. From the configuration of neurons and hidden layers to activation functions, the reader could see how Scikit-Learn supports simple neural networks, facilitating learning. The importance of normalizing data and the need to be careful with convergence issues when adjusting parameters like max_iter and alpha were discussed. This chapter emphasizes that although neural networks have become popular, it is vital to understand their operation and not just apply them indiscriminately.

Continuing, Chapter 14 explored clustering algorithms, a fundamental topic in exploratory data analysis. K-Means, DBSCAN, and Agglomerative Clustering were emphasized, each offering different ways to group samples without predefined labels. It was observed how choosing the number of clusters or the eps value in DBSCAN can drastically alter results. The message here is that there is no universal approach: it is necessary to test and evaluate which algorithm best fits the objectives.

Chapter 15 showed how dimensionality reduction can simplify data representation, facilitating both interpretation and model training. PCA and t-SNE stood out as popular techniques, although they have different objectives. PCA seeks projections that maximize variance, while t-SNE focuses on preserving local relationships. Common errors, such as information loss or slowness in t-SNE, were addressed along with recommended solutions.

Anomaly detection was the theme of Chapter 16, showing how algorithms like Isolation Forest, Local Outlier Factor, and One-Class SVM can identify points outside the expected pattern. The application of these techniques in fraud detection and cybersecurity was emphasized. The importance of properly defining contamination and other parameters was also highlighted, as incorrect adjustments can generate many false positives or ignore real anomalies.

In Chapter 17, pipeline automation gained importance. Creating pipelines in Scikit-Learn allows combining different steps (preprocessing, feature selection, final model) into a cohesive and replicable flow. It was mentioned how this approach facilitates cross-validation, hyperparameter tuning, and process standardization, reducing the chances of human error when applying transformations to test or production data.

Chapter 18 focused on deploying Scikit-Learn models, a fundamental step to take Machine Learning solutions from the development environment to production. Serialization methods like pickle and joblib, creating REST APIs with Flask or FastAPI, and the need to monitor model performance in production were addressed. This process ensures that the developed intelligence effectively reaches the end-user in a scalable way.

Then, Chapter 19 discussed handling imbalanced data, a frequent challenge in fraud detection, medical diagnoses, and other cases where one class is much rarer than the other. Techniques like oversampling (SMOTE), undersampling, and adjusting weights in the algorithm proved essential to prevent the model from ignoring the minority class. The reader could see how accuracy can be misleading in these scenarios, demanding appropriate metrics like recall and F1-score.

In Chapter 20, integration with other libraries was explored, mainly with Pandas, NumPy, and Matplotlib. The objective was to demonstrate how these tools complement Scikit-Learn in a complete data analysis, visualization, and modeling workflow. It was also mentioned how Seaborn can enrich exploratory analysis and results presentation, emphasizing the need for a cohesive ecosystem to develop truly effective solutions.

Moving forward, Chapter 21 presented automation and AutoML, highlighting frameworks like Auto-sklearn and TPOT. These tools aim to optimize algorithm selection, hyperparameter tuning, and feature engineering automatically. Thus, the data scientist can save time and focus efforts on result analysis without neglecting the need for careful data curation to avoid bias or missing data issues.

Chapter 22, about model interpretability (Explainability), emphasized the importance of explaining how the model arrived at certain predictions, addressing techniques like SHAP and LIME. This chapter is essential in scenarios where regulations or stakeholders require transparency. The ability to interpret models also helps detect possible flaws or biases, contributing to a responsible and trustworthy AI adoption.

Then, Chapter 23 dealt with Big Data integration, showing how Spark and Dask can be used to handle massive volumes of data that exceed the memory of a single machine. The reader could see how to use Spark MLlib or Dask-ML to train distributed models in clusters, ensuring scalability and avoiding computational bottlenecks. The main message was: even though Scikit-Learn is geared towards a "standard" scenario, there are ways to extend its applicability to much larger contexts.

Chapter 24 discussed MLOps and CI/CD for Scikit-Learn models, a step beyond simply creating algorithms. This topic clarified how to automate the Machine Learning lifecycle, from data collection and preprocessing, through continuous training and validation, to deployment and monitoring in production. Continuous Integration and Continuous Deployment (CI/CD) allow teams to keep model development always updated and agile, quickly responding to changes in data or business demands.

Finally, Chapter 25 presented advanced testing and debugging techniques in Machine Learning. Here, it was shown how to use pytest to create unit tests, how to verify model robustness, and how to profile resource consumption, ensuring that everything works properly when the system is in production. Debugging is not limited to finding bugs in code but also diagnosing why the model fails or consumes too much memory. This chapter crowns the idea that developing Machine Learning solutions goes far beyond writing quick scripts: every detail matters, and every part of the pipeline must be carefully designed, tested, and maintained.

Cordially,
Diego Rodrigues & Team

www.ingramcontent.com/pod-product-compliance
Lightning Source LLC
LaVergne TN
LVHW051231050326
832903LV00028B/2354